EXTREME CARNIVORE

DELICIOUSLY MEATY RECIPES

Publications International, Ltd.

Photograph on front cover and page 139 © Shutterstock.com.

Pictured on the front cover: Favorite Barbecue Ribs *(page 138)*.

Pictured on the back cover *(clockwise from top left):* Beer-Brined Pork Chops *(page 144)*, Smothered Beef and Sausage Meatball Sandwiches *(page 96)* and Chili Cheese Fries *(page 29)*.

ISBN: 978-1-63938-547-8

Manufactured in China.

8 7 6 5 4 3 2 1

Microwave Cooking: Microwave ovens vary in wattage. Use the cooking times as guidelines and check for doneness before adding more time.

Let's get social!
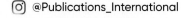
@Publications_International
@PublicationsInternational
www.pilbooks.com

CONTENTS

BREAKFAST SAUSAGE MONKEY MUFFINS
MAKES 8 MUFFINS

8 ounces bulk pork sausage

1 egg, beaten

1 cup (4 ounces) shredded Mexican cheese blend, divided

1 package (12 ounces) refrigerated buttermilk biscuits (10 biscuits)

1 Preheat oven to 350°F. Spray 8 standard (2½-inch) muffin cups with nonstick cooking spray.

2 Cook sausage in large skillet over medium-high heat 8 minutes or until no longer pink, stirring to break up meat. Spoon sausage and drippings into large bowl; let cool 2 minutes. Stir in egg until blended. Reserve 2 tablespoons cheese for tops of muffins; stir remaining cheese into sausage mixture.

3 Separate biscuits; cut each biscuit into 6 pieces with scissors. Roll biscuit pieces in sausage mixture to coat; place 7 to 8 biscuit pieces in each muffin cup. Sprinkle with reserved 2 tablespoons cheese.

4 Bake 22 minutes or until golden brown. Remove muffins to paper towel-lined plate. Serve warm.

INDIVIDUAL SPINACH AND BACON QUICHES
MAKES 12 SERVINGS

3 slices bacon

½ small onion, diced

1 package (10 ounces) frozen chopped spinach, thawed and squeezed dry

½ teaspoon black pepper

⅛ teaspoon ground nutmeg

Pinch of salt

3 eggs

1 container (15 ounces) whole-milk ricotta cheese

2 cups (8 ounces) shredded mozzarella cheese

1 cup grated Parmesan cheese

1 Preheat oven to 350°F. Spray 12 standard (2½-inch) muffin cups with nonstick cooking spray.

2 Cook bacon in large skillet over medium-high heat until crisp. Drain on paper towel-lined plate until cool enough to handle. Crumble bacon.

3 Heat same skillet with bacon drippings over medium heat. Add onion; cook and stir 5 minutes or until softened. Add spinach, pepper, nutmeg and salt; cook and stir 3 minutes or until liquid is evaporated. Remove from heat. Stir in bacon; set aside to cool.

4 Beat eggs in large bowl. Add ricotta, mozzarella and Parmesan; beat until well blended. Add spinach mixture; mix well. Spoon evenly into prepared muffin cups.

5 Bake 40 minutes or until set. Cool in pan 10 minutes. Run thin knife around edges to remove quiches from pan. Serve warm or at room temperature.

CHICKEN AND WAFFLES WITH SRIRACHA MAPLE SYRUP
MAKES 4 TO 6 SERVINGS

CHICKEN

- ½ cup milk
- 1 egg
- 1¼ pounds chicken tenders (about 8 pieces)
- 1½ cups panko bread crumbs
- 1 teaspoon salt
- 1 teaspoon garlic powder
- 1 teaspoon paprika
- ½ teaspoon black pepper
- ¼ cup vegetable oil

WAFFLES

- 2 cups pancake and baking mix
- 1⅓ cups milk
- 1 egg

SRIRACHA MAPLE SYRUP

- ½ cup maple syrup
- 2 teaspoons sriracha sauce

1 Beat ½ cup milk and 1 egg in shallow dish until blended. Add chicken; stir to coat.

2 Combine panko, salt, garlic powder, paprika and pepper in another shallow dish. Working with one piece at a time, coat chicken with panko mixture, pressing lightly to adhere. Remove to plate.

3 Heat oil in large skillet over medium-high heat. Add chicken; cook over medium heat about 6 minutes per side or until golden brown and no longer pink in center. Remove to clean plate; tent with foil to keep warm.

4 Preheat waffle maker to medium; spray with nonstick cooking spray. Combine baking mix, milk and 1 egg in medium bowl; mix well.

5 Pour ¾ cup batter into waffle maker; cook 3 to 4 minutes or until golden brown. Remove waffle to serving plate. Repeat with remaining batter.

6 Combine maple syrup and sriracha in small bowl; mix well. Serve waffles topped with chicken; drizzle with syrup.

BACON AND EGG CUPS
MAKES 12 SERVINGS

12 slices bacon, crisp-cooked and cut crosswise into thirds

6 eggs

½ cup diced red and green bell pepper

½ cup (2 ounces) shredded pepper Jack cheese

½ cup half-and-half

¼ teaspoon salt

¼ teaspoon black pepper

1 Preheat oven to 350°F. Lightly spray 12 standard (2½-inch) muffin cups with nonstick cooking spray.

2 Place three bacon slices in each prepared muffin cup, overlapping in bottom. Beat eggs, bell pepper, cheese, half-and-half, salt and black pepper in medium bowl until well blended. Fill each muffin cup with ¼ cup egg mixture.

3 Bake 20 to 25 minutes or until eggs are set in center. Run knife around edge of each cup before removing from pan.

BACON–CHEESE GRITS
MAKES 4 SERVINGS

2 cups milk

½ cup quick-cooking grits

1½ cups (6 ounces) shredded sharp Cheddar cheese *or* 6 slices American cheese, torn into bite-size pieces

2 tablespoons butter

1 teaspoon Worcestershire sauce

½ teaspoon salt

⅛ teaspoon ground red pepper (optional)

4 slices thick-cut bacon, crisp-cooked and chopped

1 Bring milk to a boil in large saucepan over medium-high heat. Slowly stir in grits; return to a boil. Reduce heat to low; cover and simmer 5 minutes, stirring frequently.

2 Remove from heat; stir in cheese, butter, Worcestershire sauce, salt and red pepper, if desired. Cover and let stand 2 minutes or until cheese is melted. Top with bacon.

TIP

For a thinner consistency, add an additional ½ cup milk.

BREAKFAST BISCUIT BAKE
MAKES 8 SERVINGS

8 ounces bacon, chopped

1 small onion, finely chopped

1 clove garlic, minced

¼ teaspoon red pepper flakes

5 eggs

¼ cup milk

½ cup (2 ounces) shredded white Cheddar cheese, divided

¼ teaspoon salt

⅛ teaspoon black pepper

1 package (16 ounces) refrigerated jumbo buttermilk biscuits (8 biscuits)

1 Preheat oven to 425°F. Cook bacon in large cast iron skillet until crisp. Remove to paper towel-lined plate. Drain off and reserve drippings, leaving 1 tablespoon in skillet.

2 Add onion, garlic and red pepper flakes to skillet; cook and stir over medium heat 4 minutes or until onion is softened. Set aside to cool slightly.

3 Beat eggs, milk, ¼ cup cheese, salt and black pepper in medium bowl until well blended. Stir in onion mixture.

4 Wipe out any onion mixture remaining in skillet; grease with additional drippings, if necessary. Separate biscuits and arrange in single layer in bottom of skillet. (Bottom of skillet should be completely covered.)

5 Pour egg mixture over biscuits; sprinkle with remaining ¼ cup cheese and cooked bacon.

6 Bake 25 minutes or until puffed and golden brown. Serve warm.

CARAMELIZED BACON
MAKES 6 SERVINGS

12 slices (about 12 ounces) applewood-smoked bacon

½ cup packed brown sugar

2 tablespoons water

¼ to ½ teaspoon ground red pepper

1 Preheat oven to 375°F. Line 15×10-inch rimmed baking sheet with foil. Spray wire rack with nonstick cooking spray; place on prepared baking sheet.

2 Arrange bacon in single layer on prepared wire rack. Combine brown sugar, water and red pepper in small bowl; mix well. Brush mixture generously over bacon.

3 Bake 20 to 25 minutes or until bacon is well browned. Immediately remove to serving platter; cool completely.

SMOKED SAUSAGE AND RED PEPPER FRITTATA
MAKES 4 SERVINGS

2 teaspoons olive oil

8 ounces smoked sausage, halved lengthwise and cut crosswise into ¼-inch slices

1 medium red bell pepper, diced

1 medium yellow squash, sliced

½ cup finely chopped onion

4 eggs

3 ounces cream cheese

½ teaspoon salt

¼ teaspoon black pepper

Salsa (optional)

1 Heat oil in large nonstick skillet over medium-high heat. Add sausage; cook and stir 4 to 5 minutes or until beginning to brown. Remove to plate.

2 Add bell pepper, squash and onion to skillet; cook and stir 4 minutes or until onion is translucent.

3 Meanwhile, combine eggs, cream cheese, salt and black pepper in blender; blend until smooth.

4 Reduce heat to medium-low; stir sausage back into skillet. Pour egg mixture over vegetables and sausage; cover and cook 10 minutes or until almost set. Remove from heat, let stand uncovered 3 minutes. Cut into quarters; serve with salsa, if desired.

OVERNIGHT BACON, SOURDOUGH, EGG AND CHEESE CASSEROLE
MAKES 6 SERVINGS

8 slices thick-cut bacon, chopped

1 large onion, chopped

1 medium red bell pepper, chopped

1 medium green bell pepper, chopped

2 teaspoons dried oregano

¼ cup sun-dried tomatoes packed in oil, drained and chopped

1 loaf (about 12 ounces) sourdough bread, cut into ¾-inch cubes

1½ cups (6 ounces) shredded sharp Cheddar cheese, divided

10 eggs

1 cup milk

1 teaspoon salt

¾ teaspoon black pepper

SLOW COOKER DIRECTIONS

1 Spray inside of slow cooker with nonstick cooking spray. Cook and stir bacon in large skillet over medium heat 7 to 9 minutes or until crisp. Drain on paper-towel lined plate. Drain all but 1 tablespoon drippings from skillet.

2 Add onion, bell peppers and oregano to skillet; cook over medium heat 5 minutes or until softened, stirring occasionally. Stir in sun-dried tomatoes; cook 1 minute.

3 Transfer mixture to slow cooker. Stir in bacon, bread and 1 cup cheese.

4 Beat eggs, milk, salt and black pepper in large bowl until well blended. Pour over bread mixture in slow cooker; press down on bread to allow bread mixture to absorb egg mixture. Sprinkle with remaining ½ cup cheese.

5 Cover; cook on LOW 8 to 10 hours or on HIGH 4 to 5 hours. Cut into squares.

CHORIZO HASH
MAKES 4 SERVINGS

2 unpeeled russet potatoes, cut into ½-inch pieces

3 teaspoons salt, divided

8 ounces uncooked Mexican chorizo sausage

1 yellow onion, chopped

½ red bell pepper, chopped (about ½ cup)

Fried, poached or scrambled eggs (optional)

Avocado slices (optional)

Fresh cilantro leaves (optional)

1 Fill medium saucepan half full with water. Add potatoes and 2 teaspoons salt; bring to a boil over high heat. Reduce heat to medium-low; cook 8 minutes. (Potatoes will be firm.) Drain.

2 Meanwhile, remove and discard casing from chorizo. Crumble chorizo into large (12-inch) cast iron skillet; cook and stir over medium-high heat 5 minutes or until lightly browned. Add onion and bell pepper; cook and stir 4 minutes or until vegetables are softened.

3 Stir in potatoes and remaining 1 teaspoon salt; cook 10 to 15 minutes or until vegetables are tender and potatoes are lightly browned, stirring occasionally. Serve with eggs, if desired; garnish with avocado and cilantro.

HAM AND CHEESE BREAD PUDDING
MAKES 8 SERVINGS

1 small loaf (8 ounces) sourdough, country French or Italian bread, sliced

3 tablespoons butter, softened

8 ounces ham or smoked ham, cubed

1 cup (4 ounces) shredded Cheddar cheese

3 eggs

2 cups milk

1 teaspoon ground mustard

½ teaspoon salt

⅛ teaspoon white pepper

1 Spray 11×7-inch baking dish with nonstick cooking spray. Spread one side of each bread slice with butter. Cut bread into 1-inch cubes; place in prepared baking dish. Top with ham; sprinkle with cheese.

2 Beat eggs in medium bowl. Add milk, mustard, salt and pepper; beat until well blended. Pour evenly over bread mixture; cover and refrigerate at least 6 hours or overnight.

3 Preheat oven to 350°F. Bake, uncovered, 45 to 50 minutes or until puffed and golden brown and knife inserted into center comes out clean. Serve immediately.

MAPLE BACON MONKEY BREAD
MAKES 12 SERVINGS

10 slices bacon, cooked and coarsely chopped (about 12 ounces)

⅓ cup packed brown sugar

¼ teaspoon black pepper

3 tablespoons butter

3 tablespoons maple syrup

1 loaf (16 ounces) frozen bread dough, thawed according to package directions

1 Spray 12-cup (10-inch) bundt pan with nonstick cooking spray.

2 Combine bacon, brown sugar and pepper in large bowl. Combine butter and maple syrup in medium microwavable bowl; microwave on HIGH 30 seconds. Stir mixture; microwave 20 seconds or until butter is melted.

3 Roll 1-inch pieces of dough into balls. Dip balls in butter mixture; roll in bacon mixture to coat. Layer in prepared pan.

4 Reheat any remaining butter mixture, if necessary; drizzle over top of dough. Cover and let rise in warm place about 45 minutes or until doubled in size. Preheat oven to 350°F.

5 Bake 30 to 35 minutes or until golden brown. Cool in pan on wire rack 5 minutes. Loosen edge of bread with knife; invert onto serving plate. Serve warm.

SAUSAGE APPLE QUICHE
MAKES 6 SERVINGS

1 unbaked deep-dish 9-inch pie crust

8 ounces bulk spicy pork sausage

½ cup chopped onion

¾ cup shredded peeled tart apple

1 tablespoon lemon juice

1 tablespoon sugar

⅛ teaspoon red pepper flakes

1 cup (4 ounces) shredded Cheddar cheese

1½ cups half-and-half

3 eggs

¼ teaspoon salt

Dash black pepper

1 Preheat oven to 450°F. Line crust with foil; partially fill with uncooked beans or rice. Bake 10 minutes. Remove foil and beans; bake crust 5 minutes or until lightly browned. Cool on wire rack. *Reduce oven temperature to 375°F.*

2 Crumble sausage into large skillet; add onion. Cook and stir over medium heat about 8 minutes or until sausage is browned and onion is tender. Drain off drippings.

3 Add apple, lemon juice, sugar and red pepper flakes; cook and stir 4 minutes or until apple is barely tender and liquid is evaporated. Remove from heat; set aside to cool slightly. Spoon sausage mixture into crust; sprinkle with cheese.

4 Beat half-and-half, eggs, salt and black pepper in medium bowl until well blended. Pour over sausage mixture in crust.

5 Bake 35 to 45 minutes or until filling is puffed and knife inserted into center comes out clean. Let stand 10 minutes before serving.

BRATWURST SKILLET BREAKFAST

MAKES 4 SERVINGS

1½ pounds red potatoes

3 bratwurst links (about 12 ounces), cut into ½-inch slices

2 tablespoons butter

1½ teaspoons caraway seeds

4 cups shredded red cabbage

1 Cut potatoes into ¼- to ½-inch pieces. Place in shallow microwavable dish; cover and microwave on HIGH 3 minutes. Stir; microwave 2 minutes or just until potatoes are tender.

2 Cook sausage in large skillet over medium-high heat 8 minutes or until browned and cooked through, stirring occasionally. Drain on paper towel-lined plate. Drain off drippings.

3 Melt butter in same skillet. Add potatoes and caraway seeds; cook 6 to 8 minutes or until potatoes are tender and golden brown, stirring occasionally.

4 Return bratwurst to skillet. Stir in cabbage; cover and cook 3 minutes or until cabbage is slightly wilted. Uncover; cook and stir 3 to 4 minutes or just until cabbage is tender.

BACON AND EGG BAKE
MAKES 4 TO 6 SERVINGS

1 package (about 12 ounces) bacon, chopped

1 onion, chopped

1 jalapeño pepper, seeded and chopped

1 clove garlic, minced

10 eggs

½ cup milk

¼ teaspoon salt

1 cup (4 ounces) shredded Italian blend or Mexican blend cheese, divided

1 Preheat oven to 350°F. Spray 8-inch square baking pan with nonstick cooking spray.

2 Cook bacon in large skillet over medium heat until crisp. Drain on paper towel-lined plate. Drain all but 1 tablespoon drippings. Add onion to skillet; cook and stir 5 minutes or until softened. Add jalapeño and garlic; cook and stir 1 minute. Remove from heat; set aside to cool slightly.

3 Beat eggs, milk and salt in large bowl until well blended. Reserve ¼ cup bacon; stir remaining bacon, ¾ cup cheese and onion mixture into egg mixture. Pour into prepared pan.

4 Bake 30 minutes. Sprinkle with remaining ¼ cup cheese and reserved bacon; bake 5 to 8 minutes or until cheese is melted and paring knife inserted into center comes out clean.

HAM AND EGG BREAKFAST PANINI
MAKES 2 SANDWICHES

1 tablespoon olive oil

¼ cup chopped red or green bell pepper

2 tablespoons sliced green onion

1 slice (1 ounce) smoked deli ham, chopped

2 eggs

¼ teaspoon salt

Pinch black pepper

4 slices multigrain or favorite sandwich bread

2 slices Cheddar or Swiss cheese

1 Heat oil in small nonstick skillet over medium heat. Add bell pepper and green onion; cook and stir 4 minutes or until vegetables are crisp-tender. Stir in ham.

2 Beat eggs, salt and black pepper in small bowl until well blended. Pour into skillet; cook 2 minutes or until egg mixture is almost set, stirring occasionally.

3 Heat grill pan or medium skillet over medium heat. Spray one side of each bread slice with nonstick cooking spray; turn bread over. Top 2 bread slices with 1 cheese slice and half of egg mixture. Top with remaining bread slices.

4 Cook sandwiches 2 minutes per side or until toasted, pressing down lightly with spatula. (Cover pan with lid during last 2 minutes of cooking to melt cheese, if desired.) Serve immediately.

SUPER STARTERS

CHILI CHEESE FRIES
MAKES 4 SERVINGS

1½ pounds ground beef

1 medium onion, chopped

2 cloves garlic, minced

½ cup lager

2 tablespoons tomato paste

2 tablespoons chili powder

Salt and black pepper

1 package (32 ounces) frozen French fries

1 jar (15 ounces) cheese sauce, heated

Sour cream and chopped green onions (optional)

1 Cook beef, onion and garlic in large skillet over medium-high heat 6 to 8 minutes or until browned, stirring to break up meat. Drain fat.

2 Stir in lager, tomato paste and chili powder; cook over medium-low heat 20 minutes or until most liquid has evaporated, stirring occasionally. Season with salt and pepper.

3 Meanwhile, bake French fries according to package directions.

4 Divide French fries evenly among serving bowls. Top with chili and cheese sauce; garnish with sour cream and green onions.

PEPPERONI STUFFED MUSHROOMS
MAKES 4 TO 6 SERVINGS

16 medium mushrooms

1 tablespoon olive oil

½ cup finely chopped onion

2 ounces pepperoni, finely chopped (about ½ cup)

¼ cup finely chopped green bell pepper

½ teaspoon seasoned salt

¼ teaspoon dried oregano

⅛ teaspoon black pepper

½ cup crushed buttery crackers (about 12)

¼ cup grated Parmesan cheese

1 tablespoon chopped fresh parsley, plus additional for garnish

1 Preheat oven to 350°F. Line baking sheet with foil; spray foil with nonstick cooking spray.

2 Clean mushrooms; remove stems and set aside caps. Finely chop stems.

3 Heat oil in large skillet over medium-high heat Add onion; cook and stir 2 to 3 minutes or until softened. Add mushroom stems, pepperoni, bell pepper, seasoned salt, oregano and black pepper; cook and stir 5 minutes or until vegetables are tender but not browned.

4 Remove from heat; stir in crushed crackers, cheese and 1 tablespoon parsley until blended. Spoon mixture into mushroom caps, mounding slightly in centers. Place filled caps on prepared baking sheet.

5 Bake 20 minutes or until heated through. Garnish with additional parsley.

CHORIZO QUESADILLAS
MAKES 6 SERVINGS

1 package (9 ounces) uncooked Mexican chorizo sausage, casings removed

1 cup coarsely chopped cauliflower

1 small onion, finely chopped

12 (6-inch) flour tortillas

1½ cups (6 ounces) grated chihuahua cheese

6 teaspoons vegetable oil

Salsa, guacamole and sour cream (optional)

1 Cook chorizo, cauliflower and onion in large skillet over medium-high heat 10 to 12 minutes or until cauliflower is tender, stirring frequently. Remove to bowl. Wipe out skillet with paper towel.

2 Spread ¼ cup chorizo mixture over each of six tortillas. Top with ¼ cup cheese and remaining six tortillas.

3 Heat 1 teaspoon oil in same skillet over medium-high heat. Add one quesadilla; cook 2 to 3 minutes per side or until well browned and cheese is melted. Repeat with remaining oil and quesadillas.

4 Cut quesadillas into wedges; serve with salsa, guacamole and sour cream, if desired.

NOTE

To keep cooked quesadillas warm, arrange on a baking sheet and place in a preheated 200°F oven until all the quesadillas are cooked and ready to serve.

SPICY KOREAN CHICKEN WINGS
MAKES 6 TO 8 SERVINGS

2 tablespoons peanut oil,
   plus additional for
   frying

2 tablespoons grated
   fresh ginger

½ cup reduced-sodium
   soy sauce

¼ cup cider vinegar

¼ cup honey

¼ cup chili garlic sauce

2 tablespoons
   orange juice

1 tablespoon dark
   sesame oil

18 chicken wings or
    drummettes

   Sesame seeds (optional)

1 Heat 2 tablespoons peanut oil in medium
   saucepan over medium-high heat. Add ginger;
   cook and stir 1 minute. Add soy sauce, vinegar,
   honey, chili garlic sauce, orange juice and
   sesame oil; cook and stir 2 minutes.

2 Heat 2 inches peanut oil in large heavy
   saucepan over medium-high heat to 350° to
   375°F; adjust heat to maintain temperature.

3 Pat wings dry with paper towels. Remove
   and discard wing tips. Add wings to hot
   oil; cook 8 to 10 minutes or until crisp and
   browned and chicken is cooked through.
   Remove to paper towel-lined plate.

4 Add wings to sauce; toss to coat. Sprinkle
   with sesame seeds, if desired.

BACON–WRAPPED TERIYAKI SHRIMP
MAKES 4 TO 5 SERVINGS

1 **pound large raw shrimp, peeled and deveined (with tails on)**

¼ **cup teriyaki marinade**

11 **to 12 slices bacon, cut in half crosswise**

1 Preheat oven to 425°F. Line baking sheet with foil.

2 Place shrimp in large resealable food storage bag. Add teriyaki marinade; seal bag and turn to coat. Marinate in refrigerator 15 to 20 minutes.

3 Remove shrimp from marinade; reserve marinade. Wrap each shrimp with one piece bacon. Place on prepared baking sheet; brush bacon with some of reserved marinade.

4 Bake 15 minutes or until bacon is crisp and shrimp are pink and opaque.

TIP
Do not use thick-cut bacon for this recipe, because the bacon will not be completely cooked when the shrimp are cooked through.

PORK MEATBALLS IN GARLICKY ALMOND SAUCE
MAKES 6 SERVINGS

½ cup blanched whole almonds

1 cup chicken broth

⅓ cup roasted red pepper

4 teaspoons minced garlic, divided

1 teaspoon salt, divided

½ teaspoon saffron threads (optional)

1 cup fresh bread crumbs, divided

¼ cup dry white wine or chicken broth

1 pound ground pork

¼ cup finely chopped onion

1 egg, lightly beaten

3 tablespoons minced fresh parsley

1 Preheat oven to 350°F. Line baking sheet with foil; spray foil with nonstick cooking spray.

2 For sauce, place almonds in food processor; process until finely ground. Add broth, red pepper, 2 teaspoons garlic, ½ teaspoon salt and saffron, if desired; process until smooth. Stir in ¼ cup bread crumbs.

3 Place ¾ cup bread crumbs in large bowl; sprinkle with wine and stir gently. Add pork, onion, egg, parsley, remaining 2 teaspoons garlic and ½ teaspoon salt; mix well.

4 Shape pork mixture into 24 (1-inch) balls. Arrange meatballs on prepared baking sheet, spacing about 1 inch apart. Bake about 20 minutes or until lightly browned.

5 Transfer meatballs to 1½-quart shallow baking dish. Pour sauce over meatballs; bake 25 to 30 minutes or until sauce is bubbly. Serve with toothpicks.

SPICY BEEF TURNOVERS
MAKES 10 SERVINGS

8 ounces ground beef

2 cloves garlic, minced

2 tablespoons soy sauce

1 tablespoon water

½ teaspoon cornstarch

1 teaspoon curry powder

¼ teaspoon Chinese five-spice powder

¼ teaspoon red pepper flakes

2 tablespoons minced green onion

1 package (7½ ounces) refrigerated buttermilk biscuits (10 biscuits)

1 egg

1 tablespoon water

1 Preheat oven to 400°F. Line baking sheet with parchment paper or spray with nonstick cooking spray.

2 Cook beef and garlic in medium skillet over medium-high heat until beef is no longer pink, stirring to break up meat. Drain fat.

3 Whisk soy sauce and water into cornstarch in small bowl until smooth. Add cornstarch mixture, curry powder, five-spice powder and red pepper flakes to skillet; cook and stir 30 seconds or until liquid is absorbed. Remove from heat; stir in green onion.

4 Separate biscuits; roll each biscuit into 4-inch round between two sheets of waxed paper. Spoon heaping tablespoon beef mixture onto one side of each biscuit; fold dough over filling to form semicircle. Pinch edges together to seal. Place turnovers on prepared baking sheet. Beat egg and water in small bowl; brush lightly over turnovers.

5 Bake 9 to 10 minutes or until golden brown. Serve warm or at room temperature.

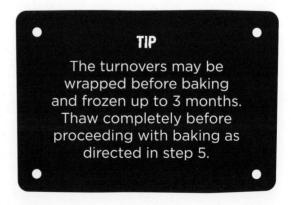

TIP

The turnovers may be wrapped before baking and frozen up to 3 months. Thaw completely before proceeding with baking as directed in step 5.

PEPPERONI PIZZA DIP WITH BREADSTICK DIPPERS
MAKES 8 SERVINGS

1 jar or can (about 14 ounces) pizza sauce

1 cup chopped pepperoni

4 green onions, chopped

1 can (2¼ ounces) sliced black olives, drained

½ teaspoon dried oregano

1 cup (4 ounces) shredded mozzarella cheese

3 ounces cream cheese, softened

Breadstick Dippers (optional, recipe follows)

SLOW COOKER DIRECTIONS

1 Combine pizza sauce, pepperoni, green onions, olives and oregano in 2-quart slow cooker; mix well.

2 Cover; cook on LOW 2 hours or on HIGH 1 to 1½ hours or until heated through.

3 Stir in mozzarella and cream cheese until cheeses are melted and well blended. Serve with Breadstick Dippers, if desired.

BREADSTICK DIPPERS

1 package (8 ounces) refrigerated breadstick dough

2 teaspoons melted butter

2 teaspoons minced fresh Italian parsley

Bake breadsticks according to package directions. Immediately after removing from oven, brush with melted butter and sprinkle with parsley.

TEX-MEX NACHOS
MAKES 4 TO 6 SERVINGS

1 tablespoon vegetable oil

8 ounces ground beef

½ cup chopped onion

2 cloves garlic, minced

2 teaspoons chili powder

1 teaspoon ground cumin

½ teaspoon salt

½ teaspoon dried oregano

1 can (about 15 ounces) kidney beans, rinsed and drained

½ cup corn

½ cup sour cream, divided

2 tablespoons mayonnaise

1 tablespoon lime juice

¼ to ½ teaspoon chipotle chili powder

½ bag tortilla chips

½ (15-ounce) jar Cheddar cheese dip, warmed

½ cup pico de gallo

¼ cup guacamole

1 cup shredded iceberg lettuce

2 jalapeño peppers, thinly sliced into rings

1 Heat oil in large skillet over medium-high heat. Add beef, onion and garlic; cook 6 to 8 minutes or until beef is no longer pink, stirring to break up meat.

2 Add chili powder, cumin, salt and oregano; cook and stir 1 minute. Stir in beans and corn. Reduce heat to medium-low; cook 5 minutes or until heated through.

3 Combine ¼ cup sour cream, mayonnaise, lime juice and chipotle chili powder in small bowl; mix well. Pour chipotle sauce into small plastic squeeze bottle.

4 Spread tortilla chips on platter or large plate. Top with beef mixture; drizzle with cheese dip. Top with pico de gallo, guacamole, remaining ¼ cup sour cream, lettuce and jalapeños. Squeeze chipotle sauce over nachos. Serve immediately.

CHICKEN BACON QUESADILLAS
MAKES 4 SERVINGS

4 teaspoons vegetable oil, divided

4 (8-inch) flour tortillas

1 cup (4 ounces) shredded Colby-Jack cheese

2 cups coarsely chopped cooked chicken

4 slices bacon, crisp-cooked and coarsely chopped

½ cup pico de gallo, plus additional for serving

Sour cream and guacamole (optional)

1 Heat large nonstick skillet over medium heat; brush with 1 teaspoon oil. Place one tortilla in skillet; sprinkle with ¼ cup cheese. Spread ½ cup chicken over one half of tortilla; top with one fourth of bacon and 2 tablespoons pico de gallo.

2 Cook 1 to 2 minutes or until cheese is melted and bottom of tortilla is lightly browned. Fold tortilla over filling, pressing with spatula. Remove to cutting board; cool slightly. Cut into wedges. Repeat with remaining ingredients.

3 Serve with additional pico de gallo, sour cream and guacamole, if desired.

SWEET AND SPICY SAUSAGE
MAKES ABOUT 16 SERVINGS

⅔ cup blackberry jam

⅓ cup steak sauce

1 tablespoon yellow mustard

½ teaspoon ground allspice

1 pound kielbasa sausage, cut diagonally into ¼-inch-thick slices

SLOW COOKER DIRECTIONS

1 Combine jam, steak sauce, mustard and allspice in slow cooker; mix well. Add sausage; stir to coat.

2 Cover; cook on HIGH 3 hours.

GREEK COFFEE MEATBALLS
MAKES ABOUT 25 LARGE MEATBALLS

1 tablespoon olive oil

1 small onion, minced

4 slices rustic bread, crusts removed and cut into ½-inch pieces

1 cup brewed coffee

1 pound ground beef

1½ tablespoons crumbled feta cheese

¼ cup chopped fresh mint

¼ cup chopped fresh Italian parsley, plus additional for garnish

2 teaspoons red wine vinegar

1 teaspoon minced fresh oregano

¾ teaspoon salt

¼ teaspoon ground pepper

½ cup finely chopped blanched almonds

½ cup all-purpose flour

Vegetable oil

1 Heat olive oil in small skillet over medium-high heat. Add onion; cook and stir over medium heat about 8 minutes or until golden brown. Set aside to cool slightly.

2 Place bread slices in medium bowl; cover with coffee and let stand until until soft. Remove bread from coffee; squeeze out excess liquid.

3 Combine cooked onion, bread, beef, cheese, mint, ¼ cup parsley, vinegar, oregano, salt and pepper in large bowl; mix gently. Cover and refrigerate at least 2 hours or overnight.

4 Shape beef mixture into golf ball-sized meatballs. Place almonds and flour in separate shallow dishes. Roll meatballs in almonds, then in flour to coat.

5 Pour vegetable oil into large skillet to depth of ½ inch; heat over medium-high heat.

6 Add meatballs in batches; cook until well browned. Drain on paper towel-lined plate. Sprinkle with additional parsley.

MINI CARNITAS TACOS
MAKES 12 SERVINGS (36 MINI TACOS)

1½ pounds boneless
    pork loin, cut into
    1-inch pieces

1 onion, finely chopped

½ cup reduced-sodium
    chicken broth

1 tablespoon chili powder

2 teaspoons ground cumin

1 teaspoon dried oregano

½ teaspoon minced
    canned chipotle
    pepper in adobo
    sauce (optional)

½ cup pico de gallo

2 tablespoons chopped
    fresh cilantro

½ teaspoon salt

12 (6-inch) corn tortillas

¾ cup (3 ounces) shredded
    sharp Cheddar cheese

Sour cream (optional)

SLOW COOKER DIRECTIONS

1 Combine pork, onion, broth, chili powder, cumin, oregano and chipotle pepper, if desired, in slow cooker; mix well.

2 Cover; cook on LOW 6 hours or on HIGH 3 hours or until pork is very tender. Pour off excess cooking liquid.

3 Shred pork with two forks; stir in pico de gallo, cilantro and salt. Cover and keep warm.

4 Cut three circles from each tortilla with 2-inch biscuit cutter. Top with pork, cheese and sour cream, if desired.

SAUSAGE ROLLS
MAKES 4 SERVINGS

8 ounces ground pork

¼ cup finely chopped
  onion

½ teaspoon coarse salt

1 teaspoon minced garlic

½ teaspoon dried thyme

½ teaspoon dried basil

¼ teaspoon dried
  marjoram

¼ teaspoon black pepper

1 sheet frozen puff pastry
  (half of 17-ounce
  package), thawed

1 egg, beaten

1 Preheat oven to 400°F. Line large baking
  sheet with parchment paper.

2 Combine pork, onion, salt, garlic, thyme,
  basil, marjoram and pepper in medium
  bowl; mix well.

3 Place puff pastry on floured surface; cut
  lengthwise into three strips at seams. Roll
  each third into 10×4½-inch rectangle. Shape
  one third of pork mixture into 10-inch log;
  arrange log along top edge of one pastry
  rectangle. Brush bottom ½ inch of rectangle
  with egg. Roll pastry down around pork; press
  to seal.

4 Cut each roll crosswise into four pieces; place
  seam side down on prepared baking sheet.
  Repeat with remaining puff pastry and pork
  mixture. Brush top of each roll with egg.

5 Bake about 25 minutes or until sausage is
  cooked through and pastry is golden brown
  and puffed. Remove to wire rack to cool
  10 minutes. Serve warm.

SUBSTANTIAL SOUPS & STEWS

STIR-FRY BEEF AND VEGETABLE SOUP
MAKES 4 SERVINGS

1 boneless beef top sirloin or top round steak (about 1 pound)

2 teaspoons dark sesame oil, divided

3 cans (about 14 ounces each) reduced-sodium beef broth

1 package (16 ounces) frozen stir-fry vegetables

3 green onions, thinly sliced

¼ cup stir-fry sauce

1 Cut beef lengthwise in half, then cut crosswise into ⅛-inch-thick strips.

2 Heat 1 teaspoon oil in large saucepan or Dutch oven over medium-high heat; tilt pan to coat bottom. Add half of beef in single layer; cook 1 minute, without stirring, or until lightly browned on bottom. Turn and cook other side about 1 minute. Remove to plate; repeat with remaining 1 teaspoon oil and beef.

3 Add broth to saucepan; bring to a boil over high heat. Add vegetables; cook over medium heat 3 to 5 minutes or until heated through. Add beef, green onions and stir-fry sauce; cook 1 minute.

CHICKEN AND SAUSAGE JAMBALAYA
MAKES 6 TO 8 SERVINGS

1½ tablespoons vegetable
    oil, divided

12 ounces boneless skinless
    chicken breast, cut
    into 1-inch pieces

12 to 14 ounces andouille
    sausage or other
    smoked sausage,
    cut into ¼-inch slices

1 onion, chopped

½ red bell pepper,
    chopped

½ green bell pepper,
    chopped

1½ tablespoons Cajun
    seasoning

3 cloves garlic, minced

¾ teaspoon dried thyme

1 can (about 14 ounces)
    diced tomatoes

2 bay leaves

½ teaspoon salt

2¾ cups chicken broth

1½ cups uncooked rice

Sliced green onions
    or chopped fresh
    parsley (optional)

1 Heat 1 tablespoon oil in large saucepan or Dutch oven over medium-high heat. Add chicken; cook about 5 minutes or until browned, stirring occasionally. Remove to plate.

2 Add remaining ½ tablespoon oil and sausage to saucepan; cook 5 minutes or until browned, stirring occasionally. Remove to plate with chicken.

3 Add onion and bell peppers to saucepan; cook 3 minutes or until vegetables are softened, scraping up browned bits from bottom of saucepan. Add Cajun seasoning, garlic and thyme; cook and stir 1 minute. Add tomatoes, bay leaves and salt; mix well. Stir in broth, rice, chicken and sausage; bring to a boil.

4 Reduce heat to low; cover and cook 30 minutes or until rice is tender and liquid is absorbed. Stir rice; remove and discard bay leaves. Top with green onions, if desired.

GUINNESS BEEF STEW
MAKES 6 SERVINGS

3 tablespoons vegetable oil, divided

3 pounds boneless beef chuck roast, cut into 1-inch pieces

2 medium onions, chopped

2 stalks celery, chopped

3 tablespoons all-purpose flour

1 tablespoon minced garlic

1 tablespoon tomato paste

2 teaspoons chopped fresh thyme

1½ teaspoons salt

½ teaspoon black pepper

1 bottle (about 15 ounces) Guinness

1 cup reduced-sodium beef broth

3 carrots, cut into 1-inch pieces

4 small turnips (12 ounces), peeled and cut into 1-inch pieces

4 medium Yukon Gold potatoes (1 pound), peeled and cut into 1-inch pieces

¼ cup finely chopped fresh parsley

1 Preheat oven to 350°F. Heat 2 tablespoons oil in Dutch oven over medium-high heat until almost smoking. Cook beef in two batches about 10 minutes or until browned, stirring occasionally. Remove to plate.

2 Add remaining 1 tablespoon oil to Dutch oven; heat over medium heat. Add onions and celery; cook about 10 minutes or until softened and onions are translucent, stirring occasionally.

3 Add flour, garlic, tomato paste, thyme, salt and pepper; cook and stir 1 minute. Stir in Guinness, scraping up browned bits from bottom of Dutch oven. Return beef to Dutch oven; stir in broth.

4 Cover and bake 1 hour. Stir in carrots, turnips and potatoes; cover and bake about 1 hour 20 minutes or until beef and vegetables are tender. Stir in parsley.

HEARTY TUSCAN SOUP
MAKES 6 TO 8 SERVINGS

1 teaspoon olive oil

1 pound bulk mild or
   hot Italian sausage*

1 medium onion, chopped

3 cloves garlic, minced

¼ cup all-purpose flour

5 cups chicken broth

1 teaspoon salt

½ teaspoon Italian
   seasoning

3 medium unpeeled
   russet potatoes
   (about 1 pound),
   halved lengthwise
   and thinly sliced

2 cups packed torn
   stemmed kale leaves

1 cup half-and-half or
   whipping cream

*Or use sausage links and
remove from casings.*

1 Heat oil in large saucepan or Dutch oven
over medium-high heat. Add sausage; cook
5 minutes or until sausage begins to brown,
stirring to break up meat.

2 Add onion and garlic; cook about 5 minutes
or until onion is softened and sausage is
browned, stirring occasionally.

3 Stir in flour until blended. Add broth, salt
and Italian seasoning; bring to a boil. Stir in
potatoes and kale. Reduce heat to medium-
low; cook 15 to 20 minutes or until potatoes
are fork-tender.

4 Reduce heat to low; stir in half-and-half. Cook
about 5 minutes or until heated through.

MEXICAN-STYLE CHILI
MAKES 6 TO 8 SERVINGS

2 pounds ground beef

2 cups finely chopped
 white onions

1 to 2 dried de arbol chiles

2 cloves garlic, minced

1 teaspoon salt

1 teaspoon ground cumin

¼ teaspoon ground cloves

1 can (28 ounces) whole
 tomatoes, undrained
 and coarsely chopped

½ cup orange juice

½ cup tequila or water

¼ cup tomato paste

1 tablespoon grated
 orange peel

 Fresh cilantro sprigs
 and lime wedges
 (optional)

1 Cook beef in large skillet over medium-high heat 6 to 8 minutes or until browned, stirring to break up meat. Drain fat. Add onions; cook and stir over medium heat 5 minutes or until tender.

2 Crush chiles into fine flakes with mortar and pestle. Add chiles, garlic, salt, cumin and cloves to skillet; cook and stir 30 seconds.

3 Stir in tomatoes with juice, orange juice, tequila, tomato paste and orange peel; bring to a boil over high heat. Reduce heat to low; cover and simmer 1½ hours, stirring occasionally.

4 Uncover skillet; cook and stir chili over medium-low heat 10 to 15 minutes or until slightly thickened. Garnish with cilantro and lime wedges.

BEEF VEGETABLE SOUP
MAKES 6 TO 8 SERVINGS

1½ pounds cubed beef
    stew meat

¼ cup all-purpose flour

3 tablespoons vegetable
    oil, divided

1 onion, chopped

2 stalks celery, chopped

3 tablespoons tomato
    paste

2 teaspoons salt

1 teaspoon dried thyme

½ teaspoon garlic powder

¼ teaspoon black pepper

6 cups beef broth, divided

1 can (28 ounces) stewed
    tomatoes, undrained

1 tablespoon
    Worcestershire sauce

1 bay leaf

4 unpeeled red potatoes
    (about 1 pound), cut
    into 1-inch pieces

3 medium carrots, cut in
    half lengthwise and
    cut into ½-inch slices

6 ounces green beans,
    trimmed and cut
    into 1-inch pieces

1 cup frozen corn

1 Combine beef and flour in medium bowl; toss to coat. Heat 1 tablespoon oil in large saucepan or Dutch oven over medium-high heat. Cook beef in two batches 5 minutes or until browned, adding additional 1 tablespoon oil after first batch. Remove beef to medium bowl.

2 Heat remaining 1 tablespoon oil in same saucepan. Add onion and celery; cook and stir 5 minutes or until vegetables are softened. Add tomato paste, salt, thyme, garlic powder and pepper; cook and stir 1 minute.

3 Stir in 1 cup broth, scraping up browned bits from bottom of saucepan. Stir in remaining 5 cups broth, tomatoes with juice, Worcestershire sauce, bay leaf and beef; bring to a boil.

4 Reduce heat to low; cover and simmer 1 hour and 20 minutes. Add potatoes and carrots; cook 15 minutes. Add green beans and corn; cook 15 minutes or until vegetables are tender. Remove and discard bay leaf before serving.

SAUSAGE AND BEAN STEW
MAKES 4 TO 6 SERVINGS

2 cups fresh bread crumbs*

2 tablespoons olive oil, divided

1 pound uncooked pork sausage, cut into 2-inch pieces

1 leek, cut in half lengthwise and thinly sliced

1 large onion, cut into quarters and cut into ¼-inch slices

1 teaspoon salt, divided

2 cloves garlic, minced

½ teaspoon dried thyme

½ teaspoon ground sage

¼ teaspoon paprika

¼ teaspoon ground allspice

¼ teaspoon black pepper

1 can (28 ounces) diced tomatoes

2 cans (about 15 ounces each) navy or cannellini beans, rinsed and drained

2 tablespoons whole grain mustard

Fresh thyme leaves (optional)

To make bread crumbs, cut 4 ounces stale baguette or country bread into several pieces; place in food processor. Pulse until coarse crumbs form.

1 Preheat oven to 350°F. Combine bread crumbs and 1 tablespoon oil in medium bowl; mix well.

2 Heat remaining 1 tablespoon oil in large ovenproof skillet over medium-high heat. Add sausage; cook 8 minutes or until browned, stirring occasionally. (Sausage will not be cooked through.) Remove to plate.

3 Add leek, onion and ½ teaspoon salt to skillet; cook 10 minutes or until vegetables are soft and beginning to brown, stirring occasionally. Add garlic; cook and stir 1 minute. Add dried thyme, sage, paprika, allspice and pepper; cook and stir 1 minute. Add tomatoes; cook 5 minutes, stirring occasionally. Stir in beans, mustard and remaining ½ teaspoon salt; bring to a simmer.

4 Return sausage to skillet, pushing down into bean mixture. Sprinkle with bread crumbs.

5 Bake 25 minutes or until bread crumbs are lightly browned and sausage is cooked through. Garnish with fresh thyme.

PASTA FAGIOLI
MAKES 8 SERVINGS

- 2 tablespoons olive oil, divided
- 1 pound ground beef
- 1 cup chopped onion
- 1 cup diced carrots (about 2 medium)
- 1 cup diced celery (about 2 stalks)
- 3 cloves garlic, minced
- 4 cups beef broth
- 1 can (28 ounces) diced tomatoes
- 1 can (15 ounces) tomato sauce
- 1 tablespoon cider vinegar
- 2 teaspoons sugar
- 1½ teaspoons dried basil
- 1¼ teaspoons salt
- 1 teaspoon dried oregano
- ¾ teaspoon dried thyme
- 2 cups uncooked ditalini pasta
- 1 can (about 15 ounces) dark red kidney beans, rinsed and drained
- 1 can (about 15 ounces) cannellini beans, rinsed and drained
- Grated Romano cheese

1 Heat 1 tablespoon oil in large saucepan or Dutch oven over medium-high heat. Add beef; cook 5 minutes or until browned, stirring to break up meat. Remove to medium bowl with slotted spoon. Drain fat.

2 Heat remaining 1 tablespoon oil in same saucepan over medium-high heat. Add onion, carrots and celery; cook and stir 5 minutes or until vegetables are tender. Add garlic; cook and stir 1 minute.

3 Stir in beef, broth, tomatoes, tomato sauce, vinegar, sugar, basil, salt, oregano and thyme; bring to a boil. Reduce heat to medium-low; cover and simmer 30 minutes.

4 Add pasta and beans; cook over medium heat 10 minutes or until pasta is tender, stirring frequently. Sprinkle with cheese.

SAUSAGE RICE SOUP
MAKES 4 TO 6 SERVINGS

2 teaspoons olive oil

8 ounces Italian sausage, casings removed

1 small onion, chopped

½ teaspoon fennel seeds

1 tablespoon tomato paste

4 cups chicken broth

1 can (about 14 ounces) whole tomatoes, undrained, crushed with hands or coarsely chopped

1½ cups water

½ cup uncooked rice

¼ teaspoon salt

⅛ teaspoon black pepper

2 to 3 ounces baby spinach

⅓ cup shredded mozzarella cheese (optional)

1 Heat oil in large saucepan or Dutch oven over medium-high heat. Add sausage; cook 8 minutes or until browned, stirring to break up meat.

2 Add onion; cook and stir 5 minutes or until softened. Add fennel seeds; cook and stir 30 seconds. Add tomato paste; cook and stir 1 minute.

3 Stir in broth, tomatoes with juice, water, rice, ¼ teaspoon salt and ⅛ teaspoon pepper; bring to a boil. Reduce heat to medium-low; cook 18 minutes or until rice is tender.

4 Stir in spinach; cook 3 minutes or until wilted. Season with additional salt and pepper. Sprinkle with cheese, if desired, just before serving.

PORK AND ANAHEIM STEW
MAKES 4 TO 6 SERVINGS

2 tablespoons olive oil, divided

1½ pounds boneless pork shoulder, trimmed and cut into ½-inch pieces

6 Anaheim peppers, cut in half lengthwise, seeded and sliced

4 cloves garlic, minced

1 pound tomatillos, papery skins removed, rinsed and chopped

2 cups chopped onions

1 can (about 15 ounces) yellow hominy, rinsed and drained

1 can (about 14 ounces) chicken broth

2 teaspoons chili powder

1½ teaspoons sugar

1 teaspoon ground cumin

1 teaspoon dried oregano

1 teaspoon liquid smoke

½ teaspoon salt

SLOW COOKER DIRECTIONS

1 Heat 1 tablespoon oil in large skillet over medium-high heat. Cook pork in batches until browned. Transfer to slow cooker.

2 Add Anaheim peppers to same skillet; cook and stir 5 minutes or until edges are well browned. Add garlic; cook and stir 30 seconds. Transfer to slow cooker.

3 Stir in tomatillos, onions, hominy, broth, chili powder, sugar, cumin and oregano; mix well.

4 Cover; cook on LOW 10 hours or on HIGH 5 hours. Stir in remaining 1 tablespoon oil, liquid smoke and salt.

BEEF BARLEY SOUP
MAKES 4 SERVINGS

1 tablespoon olive oil

12 ounces boneless beef top round steak, cut into ½-inch pieces

3 cans (about 14 ounces each) beef broth

2 cups unpeeled cubed potatoes

1 can (about 14 ounces) diced tomatoes

1 cup chopped onion

1 cup sliced carrots

½ cup uncooked pearl barley

1 tablespoon cider vinegar

2 teaspoons caraway seeds

2 teaspoons dried marjoram

2 teaspoons dried thyme

1 teaspoon salt

½ teaspoon black pepper

1½ cups sliced green beans (½-inch slices)

1 Heat oil in large saucepan over medium heat. Add beef; cook about 8 minutes or until browned on all sides, stirring occasionally.

2 Stir in broth, potatoes, tomatoes, onion, carrots, barley, vinegar, caraway seeds, marjoram, thyme, salt and pepper; bring to a boil over high heat. Reduce heat to low; cover and simmer 1½ hours.

3 Add green beans; cook, uncovered, 30 minutes or until beef is fork-tender.

CHICKEN AND SAUSAGE GUMBO
MAKES 6 SERVINGS

½ cup all-purpose flour

½ cup vegetable oil

4½ cups chicken broth

1 bottle (12 ounces) beer

3 pounds boneless skinless chicken thighs

1½ teaspoons salt, divided

½ teaspoon garlic powder

¾ teaspoon ground red pepper, divided

1 pound fully cooked andouille sausage, cut into ½-inch slices

1 large onion, chopped

½ red bell pepper, chopped

½ green bell pepper, chopped

2 stalks celery, chopped

2 cloves garlic, minced

2 bay leaves

½ teaspoon black pepper

3 cups hot cooked rice

½ cup sliced green onions

1 teaspoon filé powder (optional)

1 Add flour and oil to Dutch oven; cook over medium-low heat 20 minutes or until mixture is caramel colored, stirring frequently. (Once mixture begins to darken, watch carefully to avoid burning.)

2 Meanwhile, combine broth and beer in medium saucepan; bring to a simmer over medium-high heat. Keep warm over low heat.

3 Season chicken with ½ teaspoon salt, garlic powder and ¼ teaspoon ground red pepper.

4 Add chicken, sausage, onion, bell peppers, celery, garlic, bay leaves, black pepper, remaining 1 teaspoon salt and ½ teaspoon ground red pepper to Dutch oven; mix well. Gradually add hot broth mixture, stirring constantly to prevent lumps. Bring to a simmer; cover and simmer 1 to 2 hours.

5 Remove and discard bay leaves. Place ½ cup rice in each of six bowls; top with gumbo. Sprinkle with green onions and filé powder, if desired, before serving.

SERIOUS SANDWICHES

BLT SUPREME
MAKES 2 SERVINGS

6 to 8 slices thick-cut bacon

⅓ cup mayonnaise

1½ teaspoons minced chipotle pepper in adobo sauce

1 teaspoon lime juice

1 ripe avocado

⅛ teaspoon salt

⅛ teaspoon black pepper

4 leaves romaine lettuce

½ baguette, cut into 2 (8-inch) lengths *or* 2 hoagie rolls, split and toasted

6 to 8 slices tomato

1 Cook bacon in skillet or oven until crisp-chewy. Drain on paper towel-lined plate.

2 Meanwhile, combine mayonnaise, chipotle pepper and lime juice in small bowl; mix well.

3 Coarsely mash avocado in another small bowl; stir in salt and black pepper. Cut romaine leaves crosswise into ¼-inch strips.

4 For each sandwich, spread heaping tablespoon mayonnaise mixture on bottom half of baguette; top with one fourth of lettuce. Arrange 3 to 4 slices bacon over lettuce; spread 2 tablespoons mashed avocado over bacon. Drizzle with heaping tablespoon mayonnaise mixture. Top with 3 to 4 tomato slices, one fourth of lettuce and 3 to 4 slices bacon. Close sandwich with top half of baguette.

BARBECUE BEEF SANDWICHES
MAKES 4 SERVINGS

2½ pounds boneless beef chuck roast

2 tablespoons Southwest seasoning

1 tablespoon vegetable oil

1¼ cups beef broth

2½ cups barbecue sauce, divided

4 sandwich or pretzel buns, split

1⅓ cups prepared coleslaw* (preferably vinegar based)

Vinegar-based coleslaw provides a perfect complement to the rich beef. It can often be found at the salad bar, deli counter or prepared foods section of large supermarkets.

1 Sprinkle both sides of beef with Southwest seasoning. Heat oil in Dutch oven over medium-high heat. Add beef; cook 6 minutes per side or until browned. Remove to plate.

2 Add broth; cook 2 minutes, scraping up browned bits from bottom of Dutch oven. Stir in 2 cups barbecue sauce; bring to a boil. Return beef to Dutch oven; turn to coat.

3 Reduce heat to low; cover and cook 3 to 3½ hours or until beef is fork-tender, turning halfway through cooking.

4 Remove beef to large bowl; let stand until cool enough to handle. Meanwhile, cook sauce remaining in Dutch oven over high heat 10 minutes or until reduced and slightly thickened.

5 Shred beef into bite-size pieces. Stir in 1 cup reduced cooking sauce and ¼ cup barbecue sauce. Add remaining ¼ cup barbecue sauce, if desired. Fill buns with beef mixture; top with coleslaw.

SPICY PORK PO' BOYS
MAKES 4 SERVINGS

- 2 tablespoons chili powder
- 1 tablespoon salt
- 1 tablespoon onion powder
- 1 tablespoon granulated garlic
- 1 tablespoon paprika
- 1 tablespoon black pepper
- 1 teaspoon ground red pepper
- 1 pound boneless pork ribs
- ½ cup cola
- 1 tablespoon hot pepper sauce
- Dash Worcestershire sauce
- ½ cup ketchup
- 4 French rolls, split and toasted
- ½ cup prepared coleslaw

1 Combine chili powder, salt, onion powder, garlic, paprika, black pepper and red pepper in small bowl; mix well. Rub mixture over ribs, coating all sides. Cover and refrigerate at least 3 hours or overnight.

2 Preheat oven to 250°F. Place ribs in Dutch oven. Combine cola, hot pepper sauce and Worcestershire sauce in small bowl; drizzle evenly over ribs.

3 Cover and bake about 4 hours or until ribs are fork-tender. Remove ribs to large bowl.

4 Stir ketchup into liquid in Dutch oven; cook 4 to 6 minutes or until sauce has thickened, stirring frequently. Pour sauce over ribs in bowl, pulling meat apart with two forks and coating meat with sauce.

5 Serve pork on rolls with coleslaw.

VARIATION

Instead of coleslaw, top the pork with shredded lettuce, tomatoes and/or sliced pickles.

BEST BEEF BRISKET SANDWICH EVER
MAKES 8 TO 10 SERVINGS

1 beef brisket (about 3 pounds)

2 cups apple cider, divided

⅓ cup chopped fresh thyme *or* 2 tablespoons dried thyme

1 head garlic, cloves separated, crushed and peeled

2 tablespoons whole black peppercorns

1 tablespoon mustard seeds

1 tablespoon Cajun seasoning

1 teaspoon ground cumin

1 teaspoon celery seeds

1 teaspoon ground allspice

2 to 4 whole cloves

1 bottle (12 ounces) dark beer

8 to 10 sourdough sandwich rolls, split

Dijon mustard or horseradish sauce (optional)

SLOW COOKER DIRECTIONS

1 Combine brisket, ½ cup cider, thyme, garlic, peppercorns, mustard seeds, Cajun seasoning, cumin, celery seeds, allspice and cloves in large resealable food storage bag. Seal bag; turn to coat. Marinate in refrigerator overnight.

2 Place brisket and marinade in slow cooker. Stir in remaining 1½ cups cider and beer.

3 Cover; cook on LOW 10 hours or until brisket is tender.

4 Slice brisket; serve on rolls with mustard, if desired. Strain cooking liquid; drizzle over beef.

PEPPERONI PIZZA BAGELS
MAKES 4 SERVINGS

4 plain or sesame seed
   bagels

½ cup marinara sauce

1 cup (4 ounces) shredded
   mozzarella cheese

¼ cup mini pepperoni
   slices

   Dried oregano (optional)

1 Preheat oven to 400°F. Line baking sheet
  with parchment paper or foil.

2 Cut bagels in half crosswise. Spread
  1 tablespoon marinara sauce over each
  cut half; top with cheese and pepperoni.
  Place on prepared baking sheet.

3 Bake 8 to 10 minutes or until cheese is
  melted and beginning to brown. Sprinkle
  with oregano, if desired.

COLA SLOPPY JOES
MAKES 4 SERVINGS

1 pound ground beef

1 onion, finely chopped

¾ cup finely chopped
    green bell pepper

1½ tablespoons
    all-purpose flour

1 cup cola

½ cup ketchup

2 tablespoons
    white vinegar

1 tablespoon
    Worcestershire sauce

2 teaspoons dry mustard

½ teaspoon salt

½ teaspoon black pepper

4 hamburger buns

1 Cook beef, onion and bell pepper in large saucepan over medium heat 6 to 8 minutes or until browned, stirring to break up meat. Drain fat.

2 Stir in flour until blended. Stir in cola, ketchup, vinegar, Worcestershire sauce, mustard, salt and black pepper; cover and simmer over medium-low heat 25 to 30 minutes, stirring occasionally. Serve on buns.

CLASSIC PATTY MELTS
MAKES 4 SERVINGS

5 tablespoons butter, divided

2 large yellow onions, thinly sliced

¾ teaspoon plus pinch salt, divided

1 pound ground chuck (80% lean)

½ teaspoon garlic powder

½ teaspoon onion powder

¼ teaspoon black pepper

8 slices marble rye bread

½ cup Thousand Island dressing

8 slices (about 1 ounce each) deli American or Swiss cheese

1 Melt 2 tablespoons butter in large skillet over medium heat. Add onions and pinch of salt; cook 20 minutes or until onions are very soft and golden brown, stirring occasionally. Remove to small bowl; wipe out skillet with paper towel.

2 Combine beef, remaining ¾ teaspoon salt, garlic powder, onion powder and pepper in medium bowl; mix gently. Shape into four patties about the size and shape of bread slices and ¼ to ½ inch thick.

3 Melt 1 tablespoon butter in same skillet over medium-high heat. Add patties, two at a time; cook 3 minutes or until bottoms are browned, pressing down gently with spatula to form crust. Turn patties; cook 3 minutes or until browned. Remove patties to plate; wipe out skillet with paper towel.

4 Spread one side of each bread slice with dressing. Top 4 bread slices with cheese slice, patty, caramelized onions, another cheese slice and remaining bread slices.

5 Melt 1 tablespoon butter in same skillet over medium heat. Add two sandwiches to skillet; cook 4 minutes or until golden brown, pressing down with spatula to crisp bread. Turn sandwiches; cook 4 minutes or until golden brown and cheese is melted. Repeat with remaining 1 tablespoon butter and sandwiches.

MEATY CHILI DOGS
MAKES 12 SERVINGS

1 pound ground beef

4 ounces Italian sausage,
    casings removed

1 large onion, chopped

2 medium stalks celery,
    diced

1 jalapeño pepper,
    seeded and chopped

2 cloves garlic, minced

1 tablespoon chili powder

2 teaspoons sugar

1 can (28 ounces)
    diced tomatoes

1 can (about 15 ounces)
    pinto beans, rinsed
    and drained

1 can (12 ounces)
    tomato juice

1 cup water

12 hot dogs

12 hot dogs buns,
    split and toasted

1 Combine beef, sausage, onion, celery, jalapeño and garlic in Dutch oven; cook over medium heat until meat is cooked through and onion is tender, stirring to break up meat. Drain fat.

2 Stir in chili powder and sugar. Add tomatoes, beans, tomato juice and water; bring to a boil over high heat. Reduce heat to low; simmer 30 minutes, stirring occasionally.

3 Prepare grill for direct cooking over medium-high heat.

4 Grill hot dogs 5 to 8 minutes or until heated through, turning frequently. Serve hot dogs in buns; spoon about ¼ cup chili over each.

PROSCIUTTO PROVOLONE SANDWICHES
MAKES 4 SERVINGS

1 loaf French bread

4 teaspoons whole grain Dijon mustard

4 teaspoons butter

2 ounces sliced provolone cheese

4 cups spring greens (4 ounces)

8 ounces prosciutto or other thinly sliced ham

1 Cut bread crosswise into four 6-inch pieces; cut each piece in half horizontally.

2 Spread 1 teaspoon mustard on top halves of bread; spread 1 teaspoon butter on bottom halves.

3 Layer cheese, greens and prosciutto over buttered bread halves. Wrap each sandwich with plastic wrap; refrigerate until ready to serve.

NOTE

Sandwiches may be prepared one day in advance. Wrap with plastic wrap and refrigerate until ready to serve.

MU SHU PORK WRAPS
MAKES 4 SERVINGS

2 teaspoons dark sesame oil

1 red bell pepper, cut into short, thin strips

1 pork tenderloin (about 1 pound), cut into strips

1 medium zucchini or summer squash, or a combination, cut into strips

3 cloves garlic, minced

2 cups prepared coleslaw mix or shredded cabbage

2 tablespoons hoisin sauce

4 (10-inch) wraps or flour tortillas

¼ cup plum sauce

1 Heat oil in large skillet over medium-high heat. Add bell pepper; cook and stir 2 minutes.

2 Add pork, zucchini and garlic to skillet; cook and stir 4 to 5 minutes or until pork is cooked through and vegetables are crisp-tender. Add coleslaw mix; cook and stir 2 minutes or until wilted. Add hoisin sauce; cook and stir 1 minute.

3 Heat wraps according to package directions. Spread plum sauce down centers of wraps; top with pork mixture. Roll up tightly; cut diagonally in half.

FRENCH DIP SANDWICHES
MAKES 6 SERVINGS

3 pounds boneless beef chuck roast

½ teaspoon salt

½ teaspoon black pepper

1 tablespoon olive oil

2 large onions, cut into halves, then cut into ¼-inch slices

2¼ cups reduced-sodium beef broth, divided

3 tablespoons Worcestershire sauce

6 hoagie rolls, split

12 slices provolone cheese

1 Season beef with salt and pepper. Heat oil in Dutch oven over medium-high heat. Add beef; cook about 6 minutes per side or until browned. Remove to plate.

2 Add onions and ¼ cup broth to Dutch oven; cook 8 minutes or until golden brown, stirring occasionally and scraping up browned bits from bottom of pot. Remove half of onions to small bowl; set aside.

3 Stir in remaining 2 cups broth and Worcestershire sauce; mix well. Return beef to Dutch oven. Reduce heat to low; cover and cook 3 to 3½ hours or until beef is fork-tender.

4 Remove beef to large bowl; let stand until cool enough to handle. Shred into bite-size pieces. Add ⅔ cup cooking liquid; toss to coat. Pour remaining cooking liquid into small bowl for serving. Preheat broiler. Line baking sheet with foil.

5 Place rolls cut side up on prepared baking sheet; broil until lightly browned. Top bottom halves of rolls with cheese, beef and reserved onions. Serve with warm au jus for dipping.

MEXICAN PORK SANDWICHES
MAKES 8 SERVINGS

4 cloves garlic, minced

1 teaspoon black pepper

Juice of 1 lime

1 tablespoon olive oil

2 onions, thinly sliced

2 jalapeño peppers, seeded and thinly sliced

1 large pork tenderloin (about 2 pounds)

8 French rolls

Tomatillo salsa, shredded Monterey Jack cheese and chopped fresh cilantro

1 Preheat oven to 375°F. Line baking sheet with foil.

2 Combine garlic, black pepper, lime juice and oil in small bowl; mix well. Spread onions and jalapeños on prepared baking sheet; top with pork. Rub pork with oil mixture.

3 Roast pork 45 minutes or until pork is 145°F and barely pink in center. Wrap ends of foil over pork to keep warm. Let stand while preparing rolls.

4 Split rolls; place cut sides up on another baking sheet. Heat in oven 3 to 5 minutes or until lightly toasted.

5 Thinly slice pork. Serve on rolls with onions and jalapeños, salsa, cheese and cilantro.

SMOTHERED BEEF AND SAUSAGE MEATBALL SANDWICHES
MAKES 4 TO 6 SERVINGS

12 ounces sweet or hot
   Italian sausages,
   casings removed

12 ounces ground beef

1 onion, minced

⅓ cup Italian seasoned
   dry bread crumbs

⅓ cup grated Parmesan
   cheese

1 egg, beaten

¼ teaspoon black pepper

2 tablespoons olive oil

1 onion, sliced

1 red bell pepper, sliced

2 cloves garlic, minced

1 cup lager

1 tablespoon
   tomato paste

4 to 6 crusty rolls,
   split and toasted

1 Preheat oven to 350°F. Spray baking sheet with nonstick cooking spray.

2 Combine sausages, beef, minced onion, bread crumbs, cheese, egg and black pepper in medium bowl; mix gently. Shape into 16 meatballs. Place on prepared baking sheet.

3 Bake meatballs 20 minutes or until browned.

4 Meanwhile, heat oil in large skillet over medium heat. Add sliced onion, bell pepper and garlic; cook and stir 5 minutes or until softened. Stir in lager and tomato paste; bring to a boil. Add meatballs; partially cover and simmer over low heat 20 minutes or until liquid is reduced to 2 tablespoons.

5 Divide meatballs and vegetables evenly among rolls. Serve immediately.

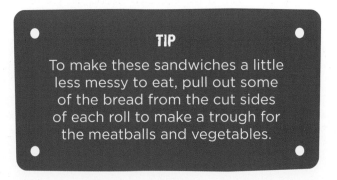

TIP
To make these sandwiches a little less messy to eat, pull out some of the bread from the cut sides of each roll to make a trough for the meatballs and vegetables.

THE ROYAL BURGER
MAKES 2 SERVINGS

1 teaspoon Royal Seasoning (recipe follows), divided

4 slices bacon

12 ounces ground beef

2 slices American cheese

2 eggs

Salt and black pepper

2 sesame seed buns, split and toasted

2 tablespoons mayonnaise

½ cup shredded lettuce

2 slices ripe tomato

1 Prepare Royal Seasoning.

2 Cook bacon in large skillet over medium heat; drain on paper towel-lined plate. Pour off all but 1 teaspoon drippings from skillet. (Reserve some bacon drippings for frying eggs, if desired.)

3 Combine beef and ¾ teaspoon Royal Seasoning in medium bowl; mix gently. Shape into two 5-inch patties. Sprinkle both sides of patties with remaining ¼ teaspoon seasoning mix.

4 Return skillet to medium heat. Cook patties 5 minutes per side or until cooked through (160°F).* Top each burger with cheese slice during last minute of cooking.

5 While burgers are cooking, heat 2 teaspoons reserved bacon drippings or butter in another large skillet or griddle over medium heat. Crack eggs into skillet; cook 3 to 4 minutes or until whites are set and yolks begin to thicken and firm around edges. Season with salt and pepper.

6 Spread cut sides of buns with mayonnaise. Top bottom halves of buns with lettuce, burgers, bacon, tomato, eggs and top halves of buns.

*Patties can also be grilled or broiled 5 minutes per side or until cooked through.

ROYAL SEASONING
MAKES ABOUT ⅓ CUP

2 tablespoons salt
1½ tablespoons paprika
1 tablespoon garlic powder
1½ teaspoons onion powder
1½ teaspoons chili powder
¾ teaspoon ground cumin
¾ teaspoon dried basil
¾ teaspoon black pepper
¼ teaspoon dried oregano

Combine salt, paprika, garlic powder, onion powder, chili powder, cumin, basil, pepper and oregano in small bowl; stir to blend. Store in airtight container. Seasoning mix can also be used for steaks, chicken and vegetables.

CAVATAPPI WITH SAUSAGE MEATBALLS
MAKES 4 SERVINGS

8 ounces uncooked cavatappi or rigatoni pasta

8 ounces bulk mild Italian sausage

8 ounces ground beef

1 onion, chopped

1 can (about 14 ounces) diced tomatoes

1 can (6 ounces) tomato paste

½ teaspoon dried oregano

¼ teaspoon salt

⅓ cup grated Parmesan cheese

1 Cook pasta according to package directions; drain and set aside.

2 Shape sausage into small marble-size meatballs. Cook meatballs in large skillet over medium-high heat about 3 minutes or until browned, stirring frequently. Remove to plate.

3 Add beef and onion to skillet; cook until beef is no longer pink, stirring to break up meat. Drain fat.

4 Return meatballs to skillet with tomatoes, tomato paste, oregano and salt; cook over medium heat 10 minutes, stirring occasionally.

5 Add pasta to skillet; stir gently to coat with sauce. Sprinkle with cheese.

CHILI AND CHEDDAR BAKED MACARONI
MAKES 8 SERVINGS

1 pound ground turkey or ground beef

1 can (8 ounces) tomato sauce

1 small onion, diced

1 jalapeño pepper, seeded and minced

1 package (1¼ ounces) chili seasoning mix

1 cup water

1 package (16 ounces) uncooked elbow macaroni

2 cups (8 ounces) shredded extra sharp Cheddar cheese

1 Cook turkey in large skillet over medium-high heat 6 to 8 minutes or until browned, stirring to break up meat. Drain fat.

2 Stir in tomato sauce, onion, jalapeño and chili seasoning. Stir in water; bring to a boil. Reduce heat to low; simmer, uncovered, about 45 minutes or until chili is thick.

3 Meanwhile, cook macaroni according to package directions until al dente. Drain well.

4 Preheat oven to 400°F. Spray 9-inch square baking dish with nonstick cooking spray. Spread one third of macaroni in baking dish; top with one third of chili and one third of cheese. Repeat layers twice.

5 Bake 30 to 35 minutes or until edges begin to brown. Let stand 5 to 10 minutes before serving.

SZECHUAN BEEF LO MEIN
MAKES 4 SERVINGS

1 boneless beef top sirloin steak (about 1 pound)

4 cloves garlic, minced

2 teaspoons minced fresh ginger

¾ teaspoon red pepper flakes, divided

1 tablespoon vegetable oil

1 can (about 14 ounces) vegetable broth

1 cup water

2 tablespoons reduced-sodium soy sauce

1 package (8 ounces) frozen mixed vegetables for stir-fry

1 package (9 ounces) refrigerated angel hair pasta

¼ cup chopped fresh cilantro (optional)

1 Cut beef in half lengthwise, then cut crosswise into thin slices. Combine beef, garlic, ginger and ½ teaspoon red pepper flakes in medium bowl; toss to coat.

2 Heat oil in large skillet or wok over medium-high heat. Add half of beef; cook and stir 2 minutes or until barely pink in center. Remove to plate; repeat with remaining beef.

3 Add broth, water, soy sauce and remaining ¼ teaspoon red pepper flakes to skillet; bring to a boil over high heat. Add vegetables; return to a boil. Reduce heat to low; cover and simmer 3 minutes or until vegetables are crisp-tender.

4 Stir in pasta; return to a boil over high heat. Reduce heat to medium; cook, uncovered, 2 minutes, separating pasta with two forks. Return beef to skillet; cook 1 minute or until pasta is tender and beef is heated through. Sprinkle with cilantro, if desired.

LITTLE ITALY BAKED ZITI
MAKES 6 TO 8 SERVINGS

1 package (16 ounces) uncooked ziti pasta

1 pound bulk mild Italian sausage

3 cloves garlic, minced

¾ cup dry white wine

1 jar (24 ounces) marinara sauce

1 can (about 14 ounces) diced tomatoes

2 tablespoons butter

2 cups (8 ounces) shredded mozzarella cheese, divided

½ cup coarsely chopped fresh basil, plus additional for garnish

¼ cup grated Parmesan cheese

1 Cook pasta in large saucepan of salted boiling water according to package directions until al dente. Drain and return to saucepan; keep warm.

2 Meanwhile, cook sausage in large skillet over medium-high heat about 8 minutes or until no longer pink, stirring to break up meat. Add garlic; cook and stir 1 minute. Add wine; cook 4 minutes or until almost evaporated.

3 Stir in marinara sauce, tomatoes and butter; bring to a boil. Reduce heat to medium-low; cook 20 minutes, stirring occasionally.

4 Preheat broiler. Spray 3-quart or 13×9-inch broilerproof baking dish with nonstick cooking spray.

5 Add sauce mixture, 1 cup mozzarella and ½ cup basil to pasta in saucepan; stir gently to coat. Spread in prepared baking dish; sprinkle with remaining 1 cup mozzarella and Parmesan.

6 Broil 2 to 3 minutes or until cheese begins to bubble and brown. Garnish with additional basil.

ORECCHIETTE WITH SAUSAGE AND BROCCOLI RABE
MAKES 4 TO 6 SERVINGS

1 tablespoon olive oil

12 ounces bulk mild Italian sausage

3 cloves garlic, minced

¼ teaspoon red pepper flakes

4 cups chicken broth, divided

¾ teaspoon salt

1 package (16 ounces) uncooked orecchiette pasta

1 bunch broccoli rabe (about 1 pound), tough stems removed, cut into 2-inch-long pieces

¾ cup grated Parmesan cheese, divided

Juice of 1 lemon

1 Heat oil in large saucepan or Dutch oven over medium-high heat. Add sausage; cook about 8 minutes or until browned, stirring to break up meat.

2 Add garlic and red pepper flakes; cook and stir 1 minute. Add 2 tablespoons broth, cook 1 minute, scraping up browned bits from bottom of saucepan.

3 Stir in remaining broth and salt; bring to a boil. Add pasta, stirring to separate pieces as much as possible. (Orecchiette pasta often sticks together in stacks in the package and during cooking.) Reduce heat to medium; cover and cook 10 minutes, stirring occasionally to prevent pasta from sticking.

4 Add broccoli rabe; stir to wilt and blend with pasta. Cover and cook 4 minutes or until pasta is tender and liquid is absorbed, stirring occasionally.

5 Stir in ½ cup cheese and lemon juice; mix well. Serve immediately with remaining cheese.

CLASSIC LASAGNA
MAKES 6 TO 8 SERVINGS

1 tablespoon olive oil

8 ounces bulk mild Italian sausage

8 ounces ground beef

1 medium onion, chopped

3 cloves garlic, minced, divided

1½ teaspoons salt, divided

1 can (28 ounces) crushed tomatoes

1 can (28 ounces) diced tomatoes

2 teaspoons Italian seasoning

1 egg

1 container (15 ounces) ricotta cheese

¾ cup grated Parmesan cheese, divided

½ cup minced fresh parsley

¼ teaspoon black pepper

12 uncooked no-boil lasagna noodles

4 cups (16 ounces) shredded mozzarella

1 Preheat oven to 350°F. Spray 13×9-inch baking dish with nonstick cooking spray.

2 Heat oil in large saucepan over medium-high heat. Add sausage, beef, onion, 2 cloves garlic and 1 teaspoon salt; cook and stir 10 minutes or until meat is no longer pink, breaking up meat with wooden spoon.

3 Stir in crushed tomatoes, diced tomatoes and Italian seasoning; bring to a boil. Reduce heat to medium-low; cook 15 minutes, stirring occasionally.

4 Meanwhile, beat egg in medium bowl. Stir in ricotta, ½ cup Parmesan, parsley, remaining 1 clove garlic, ½ teaspoon salt and pepper until well blended.

5 Spread ¼ cup sauce in prepared baking dish. Top with three noodles, breaking to fit if necessary. Spread one third of ricotta mixture over noodles. Sprinkle with 1 cup mozzarella; top with 2 cups sauce. Repeat layers of noodles, ricotta mixture, mozzarella and sauce twice. Top with remaining three noodles, sauce, 1 cup mozzarella and ¼ cup Parmesan. Cover baking dish with foil sprayed with cooking spray.

6 Bake 30 minutes. Uncover; bake 10 to 15 minutes or until hot and bubbly. Let stand 10 minutes before serving.

SHANGHAI PORK NOODLE BOWL
MAKES 4 SERVINGS

8 ounces uncooked spaghetti, broken in half

⅓ cup teriyaki sauce

2 tablespoons rice vinegar

¼ teaspoon red pepper flakes

1 tablespoon vegetable oil

1 pound pork tenderloin, halved lengthwise and cut into ¼-inch slices

2 teaspoons olive oil

4 cups sliced bok choy

1 can (11 ounces) mandarin orange sections, drained

½ cup sliced green onions

1 Cook spaghetti according to package directions; drain and keep warm in large bowl.

2 Combine teriyaki sauce, vinegar and red pepper flakes in small bowl; mix well.

3 Heat half of oil in large skillet over medium-high heat. Add half of pork; cook and stir 2 to 3 minutes or until barely pink. Remove to plate. Repeat with remaining half of oil and pork.

4 Add bok choy to skillet; cook and stir 1 to 2 minutes or until wilted. Return pork to skillet. Stir in teriyaki mixture; cook until heated through.

5 Add pork mixture, orange sections and green onions to noodles; toss to coat.

PASTA CAMPAGNOLO
MAKES 4 SERVINGS

3 tablespoons olive oil

8 ounces Italian sausage, casings removed

1 small onion, finely chopped

1 red bell pepper, cut into ¼-inch strips

2 cloves garlic, minced

⅓ cup dry white wine

1 can (28 ounces) crushed tomatoes

1 can (8 ounces) tomato sauce

4 tablespoons chopped fresh basil, divided, plus additional for garnish

½ teaspoon salt

¼ teaspoon black pepper

⅛ teaspoon red pepper flakes

1 package (16 ounces) uncooked rigatoni or penne pasta

¼ cup grated Romano cheese

1 package (4 ounces) goat cheese, cut crosswise into 8 slices

1 Heat oil in large saucepan over medium heat. Break sausage into ½-inch pieces; add to saucepan. Cook about 5 minutes or until browned, stirring occasionally.

2 Add onion and bell pepper; cook and stir 4 minutes or until vegetables are softened. Add garlic; cook and stir 1 minute.

3 Stir in wine; cook about 5 minutes or until most of liquid has evaporated. Stir in tomatoes, tomato sauce, 2 tablespoons basil, salt, black pepper and red pepper flakes; bring to a boil. Reduce heat to medium-low; cook 20 minutes or until sauce has thickened slightly.

4 Meanwhile, cook pasta in medium saucepan of salted boiling water according to package directions until al dente. Drain pasta and add to sauce with Romano cheese and remaining 2 tablespoons basil; stir gently to coat. Cook just until heated through.

5 Top each serving with goat cheese; garnish with additional basil.

BACON LOVERS' BAKED PASTA AND CHEESE
MAKES 4 SERVINGS

8 ounces uncooked fusilli pasta or other corkscrew-shaped pasta

12 slices bacon, chopped

½ medium onion, chopped

2 cloves garlic, minced

2 teaspoons dried oregano, divided

1 can (8 ounces) tomato sauce

1 teaspoon hot pepper sauce (optional)

1½ cups (6 ounces) shredded Cheddar or Colby cheese

½ cup fresh bread crumbs (from 1 slice of white bread)

1 tablespoon butter, melted

1 Preheat oven to 400°F. Cook pasta according to package directions; drain.

2 Meanwhile, cook bacon in large ovenproof skillet over medium heat until crisp. Drain on paper towel-lined plate.

3 Add onion, garlic and 1 teaspoon oregano to skillet; cook and stir 3 minutes or until onion is translucent. Stir in tomato sauce and hot pepper sauce, if desired. Add pasta and cheese; stir to coat.

4 Combine bacon, bread crumbs, remaining 1 teaspoon oregano and butter in small bowl; sprinkle over pasta mixture. Bake 10 to 15 minutes or until hot and bubbly.

HEARTY NOODLE CASSEROLE
MAKES 4 TO 6 SERVINGS

1 pound Italian sausage, casings removed

1 jar (26 ounces) pasta sauce

2 cups (16 ounces) ricotta or cottage cheese

1 package (12 ounces) extra wide egg noodles, cooked and drained

2 cups (8 ounces) shredded mozzarella cheese, divided

1 can (4 ounces) sliced mushrooms, drained

½ cup chopped green bell pepper

1 Preheat oven to 350°F. Cook sausage in large skillet over medium-high heat 6 to 8 minutes or until browned, stirring to break up meat. Drain fat.

2 Combine sausage, pasta sauce, ricotta, noodles, 1 cup mozzarella, mushrooms and bell pepper in large bowl; mix well. Spoon into 13×9-inch or 3-quart baking dish. Top with remaining 1 cup mozzarella.

3 Bake 25 minutes or until heated through.

MEATY SAUSAGE SPAGHETTI
MAKES 6 TO 8 SERVINGS

1 tablespoon olive oil

1 cup chopped onion

2 cloves garlic, minced

1 package (20 ounces) bulk Italian sausage

1 cup chopped yellow, red and/or green bell peppers

1 can (about 14 ounces) crushed tomatoes

1 can (about 14 ounces) diced tomatoes

2½ teaspoons salt

2 teaspoons dried basil

1 teaspoon dried oregano

¼ teaspoon black pepper

1 package (16 ounces) uncooked spaghetti, broken in half

2½ to 3 cups water, divided

Grated Parmesan cheese

1 Heat oil in large saucepan or Dutch oven over medium-high heat. Add onion and garlic; cook and stir 3 minutes or until softened. Add sausage; cook about 8 minutes or until browned, stirring to break up meat. Drain fat.

2 Add bell peppers to saucepan; cook and stir 2 minutes. Add crushed tomatoes, diced tomatoes, salt, basil, oregano and pepper; mix well.

3 Add pasta to saucepan; stir gently to allow some liquid to get between strands of spaghetti to prevent sticking. Add 2½ cups water; bring to a boil. Reduce heat to medium; cover and cook 15 minutes, stirring occasionally.

4 Uncover; add additional water if pasta seems dry. Test for doneness; continue to cook 2 to 3 minutes or until pasta reaches desired doneness, stirring frequently. Season with additional salt and pepper. Serve immediately with cheese.

VARIATION

You can substitute 1 pound of ground beef, ground pork or meatloaf mix for the sausage.

PIZZA CASSEROLE
MAKES 6 SERVINGS

2 cups uncooked rotini or other spiral pasta

1½ pounds ground beef

1 medium onion, chopped

Salt and black pepper

1 can (about 15 ounces) pizza sauce

1 can (8 ounces) tomato sauce

1 can (6 ounces) tomato paste

½ teaspoon sugar

½ teaspoon garlic salt

½ teaspoon dried oregano

2 cups (8 ounces) shredded mozzarella cheese

12 to 15 slices pepperoni

1 Preheat oven to 350°F. Cook pasta according to package directions; drain.

2 Meanwhile, cook beef and onion in large ovenproof skillet over medium-high heat 6 to 8 minutes or until browned, stirring to break up meat. Drain fat. Season with salt and pepper.

3 Combine pasta, pizza sauce, tomato sauce, tomato paste, sugar, garlic salt and oregano in large bowl; mix well. Add beef mixture; stir until blended.

4 Spread half of mixture in ovenproof skillet or 3-quart casserole; top with 1 cup cheese. Repeat layers. Top with pepperoni.

5 Bake 25 to 30 minutes or until heated through and cheese is melted.

SPICY SMOKED BEEF RIBS
MAKES 4 TO 6 SERVINGS

4 wood chips for smoking

4 to 6 pounds beef back ribs, cut into 3- to 4-rib portions

  Black pepper

1⅓ cups barbecue sauce

2 teaspoons hot pepper sauce or Szechuan chili sauce

  Beer, at room temperature, or hot water

1 Soak wood chips in water at least 30 minutes; drain.

2 Spread ribs on large baking sheet; season with black pepper. Combine barbecue sauce and hot pepper sauce in small bowl. Brush ribs with half of sauce. Marinate in refrigerator 30 minutes to 1 hour.

3 Prepare grill for indirect cooking over low heat. (Maintain cooking temperature at 250° to 275°F.) Add soaked wood chips to fire. Place foil drip pan in center of grill; fill pan half full with beer.

4 Place ribs on grid, meaty side up, directly above drip pan. Grill ribs, covered, 1 hour or until meat is tender, brushing remaining sauce over ribs 2 or 3 times during cooking.

GRILLED PORK CHOPS WITH LAGER BARBECUE SAUCE
MAKES 4 SERVINGS

1 cup lager

⅓ cup maple syrup

3 tablespoons molasses

1 teaspoon Mexican-style hot chili powder

4 bone-in center-cut pork chops (about 1 inch thick and 8 ounces each)

Lager Barbecue Sauce (recipe follows)

¾ teaspoon salt

¼ teaspoon black pepper

1 Combine lager, maple syrup, molasses, chili powder in medium bowl; mix well. Place pork chops in large resealable food storage bag. Pour marinade over pork chops; seal bag and turn to coat. Marinate in refrigerator 2 hours, turning occasionally.

2 Prepare Lager Barbecue Sauce.

3 Prepare grill for direct cooking over medium-high heat. Oil grid. Remove pork chops from marinade; discard marinade. Sprinkle with salt and pepper.

4 Grill pork chops 5 to 6 minutes per side or until pork is 145°F. Serve with barbecue sauce.

LAGER BARBECUE SAUCE
MAKES ABOUT ½ CUP

½ cup lager

⅓ cup ketchup

3 tablespoons maple syrup

2 tablespoons finely chopped onion

1 tablespoon molasses

1 tablespoon cider vinegar

½ teaspoon Mexican-style hot chili powder

Combine lager, ketchup, maple syrup, onion, molasses, vinegar and chili powder in small saucepan; bring to a simmer over medium heat. Cook 10 to 12 minutes or until slightly thickened, stirring occasionally.

STEAK AL FORNO
MAKES 2 TO 3 SERVINGS

4 cloves garlic, minced

1 tablespoon olive oil

1 tablespoon coarse salt

1 teaspoon black pepper

2 porterhouse or T-bone steaks (1 to 1¼ inches thick)

¼ cup grated Parmesan cheese (optional)

1 Prepare grill for direct cooking over medium-high heat.

2 Combine garlic, oil, salt and pepper in small bowl; press into both sides of steaks. Let stand 15 minutes.

3 Grill steaks, covered, 7 to 10 minutes per side for medium rare (135°F) or to desired doneness. Sprinkle with cheese, if desired, during last minute of cooking.

4 Transfer to cutting board; tent with foil and let stand 5 minutes. To serve, cut meat away from each side of bone. Cut boneless pieces into slices. Serve immediately.

TIP

For a smoked flavor, soak 2 cups hickory or oak wood chips in cold water to cover at least 30 minutes. Drain and scatter over hot coals before grilling.

KOREAN BEEF SHORT RIBS
MAKES 4 TO 6 SERVINGS

2½ pounds beef chuck flanken-style short ribs, cut ⅜ to ½ inch thick*

¼ cup chopped green onions

¼ cup water

¼ cup soy sauce

1 tablespoon sugar

2 teaspoons grated fresh ginger

2 teaspoons dark sesame oil

2 cloves garlic, minced

½ teaspoon black pepper

1 tablespoon sesame seeds, toasted**

Flanken-style ribs can be ordered from your butcher. They are cross-cut short ribs sawed through the bones.

**To toast sesame seeds, spread seeds, cook in small skillet over medium-low heat 3 minutes or until seeds begin to pop and turn golden, shaking frequently.*

1 Place ribs in large resealable food storage bag. Combine green onions, water, soy sauce, sugar, ginger, oil, garlic and pepper in small bowl; mix well. Pour over ribs; seal bag and turn to coat. Marinate in refrigerator at least 4 hours or up to 8 hours, turning occasionally.

2 Prepare grill for direct cooking over medium-high heat. Remove ribs from marinade; reserve marinade.

3 Grill ribs, covered, 5 minutes. Brush lightly with reserved marinade; turn and brush again. Discard remaining marinade. Grill, covered, 5 to 6 minutes or until ribs are well browned. Sprinkle with sesame seeds.

BEER–BASTED BARBECUE PORK CHOPS
MAKES 6 SERVINGS

1 cup barbecue sauce, divided

1 cup plus 3 tablespoons beer, divided

3 tablespoons honey

1 tablespoon chili powder

6 bone-in pork loin chops, (about 1 inch thick and 6 ounces each)

1 teaspoon salt

½ teaspoon black pepper

1 Combine ½ cup barbecue sauce, 1 cup beer, honey and chili powder in large bowl. Add pork chops; turn to coat. Cover and refrigerate 2 to 4 hours, turning occasionally.

2 Combine remaining ½ cup barbecue sauce and 3 tablespoons beer in small bowl; mix well.

3 Prepare grill for direct cooking over medium-high heat. Oil grid. Remove pork chops from marinade; discard marinade. Sprinkle with salt and pepper.

4 Grill pork chops 4 minutes; turn and brush with half of reserved barbecue sauce mixture. Grill 3 minutes; turn and brush with remaining sauce mixture. Grill 4 to 5 minutes or until pork is 145°F.

THAI-STYLE PORK CHOPS WITH CUCUMBER SAUCE
MAKES 4 SERVINGS

3 tablespoons Thai peanut sauce, divided

¼ teaspoon red pepper flakes

4 bone-in pork chops (5 to 6 ounces each)

1 container (6 ounces) plain yogurt

¼ cup diced unpeeled cucumber

2 tablespoons chopped red onion

2 tablespoons finely chopped fresh mint or cilantro

1 teaspoon sugar

1 Combine 2 tablespoons peanut sauce and red pepper flakes in small bowl; brush evenly over both sides of pork chops. Let stand while preparing cucumber sauce, or refrigerate up to 4 hours.

2 Combine yogurt, cucumber, onion, mint and sugar in medium bowl; mix well.

3 Prepare grill for direct cooking over medium heat.

4 Grill pork chops, covered, 4 minutes. Turn and grill 3 minutes or until pork is barely pink in center. Just before removing from heat, brush with remaining 1 tablespoon peanut sauce. Serve with cucumber sauce.

GREEK LAMB WITH TZATZIKI SAUCE
MAKES 4 SERVINGS

2½ to 3 pounds boneless leg of lamb

8 cloves garlic, divided

¼ cup Dijon mustard

2 tablespoons minced fresh rosemary

2 teaspoons salt

2 teaspoons black pepper

¼ cup plus 2 teaspoons olive oil, divided

1 small seedless cucumber

1 tablespoon chopped fresh mint

1 teaspoon lemon juice

2 cups plain Greek yogurt

1 Untie and unroll lamb to lie flat; trim fat.

2 Mince four garlic cloves; place in small bowl. Add mustard, rosemary, salt and pepper; whisk in ¼ cup olive oil until well blended.

3 Spread mustard mixture evenly over lamb, coating both sides. Place lamb in large resealable food storage bag; seal bag and refrigerate at least 2 hours or overnight, turning several times.

4 Meanwhile, prepare sauce. Mince remaining four garlic cloves and mash to a paste. Place in medium bowl. Peel and grate cucumber; squeeze to remove excess moisture. Add cucumber, mint, remaining 2 teaspoons olive oil and lemon juice to bowl with garlic. Add yogurt; mix well. Refrigerate until ready to serve.

5 Prepare grill for direct cooking over medium-high heat.

6 Grill lamb 30 to 35 minutes until 130° to 135°F for medium rare or to desired doneness. Tent with foil; let stand 5 to 10 minutes. Slice lamb; serve with sauce.

GRILLED PORK FAJITAS
MAKES 4 SERVINGS

2 cloves garlic, minced

2 teaspoons chili powder

½ teaspoon salt

½ teaspoon ground cumin

½ teaspoon ground
   coriander

1 pork tenderloin (about
   12 ounces)

1 medium red onion,
   cut into ½-inch rings

1 mango, peeled and
   cut into ½-inch pieces

8 (6-inch) flour tortillas,
   warmed

½ cup salsa verde

1 Prepare grill for direct cooking over medium-high heat. Oil grid.

2 Combine garlic, chili powder, salt, cumin and coriander in small bowl; mix well. Rub mixture all over pork.

3 Grill pork 12 to 16 minutes or until pork is 145°F, turning occasionally. Add onion to grill during last 8 minutes of cooking; grill until tender, turning occasionally.

4 Remove onion to small bowl. Remove pork to cutting board; tent with foil and let stand 5 to 10 minutes.

5 Cut pork into ½-inch strips. Divide pork, onion and mango among tortillas; top with salsa. Fold bottom 3 inches of each tortilla up over filling; roll up to enclose filling.

STEAK AND MUSHROOM SKEWERS
MAKES 4 SERVINGS

¼ cup Italian salad dressing

2 tablespoons Worcestershire sauce

1 pound beef top sirloin steak, cut into 24 (1-inch) pieces

24 medium whole mushrooms (about 12 ounces)

¼ cup mayonnaise

¼ cup sour cream

1 clove garlic, minced

¼ teaspoon salt

¼ teaspoon dried rosemary

1 medium zucchini, cut into 24 (1-inch) pieces

1 medium green bell pepper, cut into 24 (1-inch) pieces

1 Combine dressing and Worcestershire sauce in small bowl; mix well. Reserve 2 tablespoons dressing mixture; set aside.

2 Combine beef, mushrooms and remaining dressing mixture in large resealable food storage bag. Seal bag; turn to coat. Marinate in refrigerator 30 to 60 minutes.

3 Combine mayonnaise, sour cream, garlic, salt and rosemary in small bowl; mix well. Cover and refrigerate sauce until ready to use.

4 Prepare grill for direct cooking over medium-high heat. Thread beef, mushrooms, zucchini and bell pepper alternately onto eight 10-inch skewers. Discard remaining marinade.

5 Grill skewers 6 to 8 minutes for medium or to desired doneness, turning occasionally. Before serving, brush with reserved 2 tablespoons dressing mixture. Serve with sauce.

FAVORITE BARBECUE RIBS
MAKES 4 SERVINGS

1¼ cups water

1 cup white vinegar

⅔ cup packed dark
  brown sugar

½ cup tomato paste

1 tablespoon yellow
  mustard

1½ teaspoons salt

1 teaspoon liquid smoke

1 teaspoon onion powder

½ teaspoon garlic powder

½ teaspoon paprika

2 racks pork baby back
  ribs (3½ to 4 pounds
  total)

1 Combine water, vinegar, brown sugar, tomato paste, mustard, salt, liquid smoke, onion powder, garlic powder and paprika in medium saucepan; bring to a boil over medium heat. Reduce heat to medium-low; cook 40 minutes or until sauce thickens, stirring occasionally.

2 Preheat oven to 300°F. Place each rack of ribs on large sheet of heavy-duty foil. Brush some of sauce over ribs, covering completely. Fold down edges of foil tightly to seal and create packet; arrange packets on baking sheet, seam sides up.

3 Bake 2 hours. Prepare grill or preheat broiler. Carefully open foil packets and drain off excess liquid.

4 Brush ribs with sauce; grill about 5 minutes per side or until edges of ribs are charred, brushing with sauce once or twice during grilling. Serve with remaining sauce.

CUBAN GARLIC LIME PORK CHOPS
MAKES 4 SERVINGS

4 boneless pork top loin chops (about ¾ inch thick and 6 ounces each)

2 tablespoons olive oil

2 tablespoons lime juice

2 tablespoons orange juice

2 teaspoons minced garlic

½ teaspoon salt, divided

½ teaspoon red pepper flakes

2 small seedless oranges, peeled and chopped

1 medium cucumber, peeled, seeded and chopped

2 tablespoons chopped onion

2 tablespoons chopped fresh cilantro

1 Place pork chops in large resealable food storage bag. Add oil, lime juice, orange juice, garlic, ¼ teaspoon salt and red pepper flakes; seal bag and turn to coat. Marinate in refrigerator at least 1 hour or overnight.

2 Combine oranges, cucumber, onion and cilantro in medium bowl; toss gently. Cover and refrigerate 1 hour or overnight. Add remaining ¼ teaspoon salt just before serving.

3 Prepare grill for direct cooking over medium heat or preheat broiler. Remove pork chops from marinade; discard marinade.

4 Grill pork chops 6 to 8 minutes per side or until pork is barely pink in center. Serve with orange salsa.

SESAME-GARLIC FLANK STEAK
MAKES 4 SERVINGS

1 beef flank steak
   (about 1¼ pounds)

2 tablespoons soy sauce

2 tablespoons hoisin sauce

1 tablespoon dark
   sesame oil

2 cloves garlic, minced

1 Score steak lightly with sharp knife in diamond pattern on both sides; place in large resealable food storage bag.

2 Combine soy sauce, hoisin sauce, oil and garlic in small bowl; mix well. Pour over steak; seal bag and turn to coat. Marinate in refrigerator at least 2 hours or up to 24 hours, turning once.

3 Prepare grill for direct cooking over medium heat. Remove steak from marinade; reserve marinade.

4 Grill steak, covered, 13 to 18 minutes for medium rare (135°F) or to desired doneness, turning and brushing with marinade halfway through cooking time. Discard remaining marinade. Remove steak to cutting board; let rest 5 minutes. Cut across the grain into thin slices.

PEPPERED BEEF RIB EYE ROAST
MAKES 6 TO 8 SERVINGS

1½ tablespoons black
    peppercorns

1 boneless beef rib eye
    roast (about 2½ to
    3 pounds), well
    trimmed

¼ cup Dijon mustard

2 cloves garlic, minced

Sour Cream Sauce
(recipe follows)

1 Prepare grill for indirect cooking over medium heat with drip pan in center.

2 Place peppercorns in small resealable food storage bag. Squeeze out excess air; seal bag. Pound peppercorns with flat side of meat mallet or rolling pin until cracked.

3 Pat roast dry with paper towels. Combine mustard and garlic in small bowl; spread over roast. Sprinkle with pepper.

4 Place roast on grid directly over drip pan. Grill, covered, 1 hour or until 135°F for medium rare or to desired doneness. (Test for doneness with thermometer inserted into thickest part of roast.)

5 Meanwhile, prepare Sour Cream Sauce; cover and refrigerate until ready to serve.

6 Remove roast to cutting board. Tent with foil; let stand 10 to 15 minutes before carving. Serve with sauce.

SOUR CREAM SAUCE

Combine ¾ cup sour cream, 2 tablespoons prepared horseradish, 1 tablespoon balsamic vinegar and ½ teaspoon sugar in small bowl; mix well.

BEER-BRINED PORK CHOPS
MAKES 4 SERVINGS

1 bottle (12 ounces) dark beer

¼ cup packed dark brown sugar

1 tablespoon salt

1 tablespoon chili powder

2 cloves garlic, minced

3 cups ice water

4 pork chops (1 inch thick)

1 Combine beer, brown sugar, salt, chili powder and garlic in medium bowl; stir until salt is dissolved. Add ice water; stir until ice melts.

2 Add pork chops to brine; place medium plate on top to keep pork submerged. Refrigerate 3 to 4 hours.

3 Prepare grill for direct cooking over medium heat. Drain pork chops; pat dry with paper towels.

4 Grill pork chops, covered, 5 to 6 minutes per side or until pork is 145°F.

TIP

Brining adds flavor and moisture to meats. Make sure that your pork chops have not been injected with a sodium solution (check the package label) or they might end up too salty.

GRILLED STRIP STEAKS WITH CHIMICHURRI
MAKES 4 SERVINGS

Chimichurri
(recipe follows)

4 bone-in strip steaks
(about 1 inch thick
and 8 ounces each)

¾ teaspoon salt

¾ teaspoon ground cumin

¼ teaspoon black pepper

1 Prepare Chimichuri.

2 Prepare grill for direct cooking over medium-high heat. Oil grid. Sprinkle both sides of steaks with salt, cumin and pepper.

3 Grill steaks, covered, 4 to 5 minutes per side for medium rare (135°F) or to desired doneness. Serve with Chimichurri.

CHIMICHURRI
MAKES ABOUT 1 CUP

½ cup packed fresh basil

⅓ cup extra virgin olive oil

¼ cup packed fresh parsley

2 tablespoons packed
fresh cilantro

2 tablespoons lemon juice

1 clove garlic

½ teaspoon salt

½ teaspoon grated
orange peel

¼ teaspoon ground
coriander

⅛ teaspoon black pepper

Combine basil, oil, parsley, cilantro, lemon juice, garlic, salt, orange peel, coriander and pepper in food processor or blender; pulse until coarsley chopped.

SAUSAGE AND PEPPERS
MAKES 4 SERVINGS

1 pound uncooked hot
   or mild Italian sausage

2 tablespoons olive oil

3 medium onions, cut
   into ½-inch slices

2 red bell peppers, cut
   into ½-inch slices

2 green bell peppers,
   cut into ½-inch slices

1½ teaspoons coarse salt,
   divided

1 teaspoon dried oregano

Italian rolls (optional)

1 Fill medium saucepan half full with water
   or beer; bring to a boil over high heat. Add
   sausage; cook 5 minutes over medium heat.
   Drain and cut diagonally into 1-inch slices.

2 Heat oil in large skillet over medium-high
   heat. Add sausage; cook about 10 minutes
   or until browned, stirring occasionally.
   Remove sausage to plate; set aside.

3 Add onions, bell peppers, 1 teaspoon salt
   and oregano to skillet; cook over medium
   heat about 25 minutes or until vegetables
   are very soft and browned in spots, stirring
   occasionally.

4 Stir sausage and remaining ½ teaspoon salt
   into skillet; cook 3 minutes or until heated
   through. Serve with rolls, if desired.

MEATBALLS AND RICOTTA
MAKES 5 TO 6 SERVINGS (20 MEATBALLS)

MEATBALLS

2 tablespoons olive oil

½ cup plain dry
bread crumbs

½ cup milk

1 cup finely chopped
yellow onion

2 green onions,
finely chopped

½ cup grated Romano
cheese, plus additional
for serving

2 eggs, beaten

¼ cup finely chopped
fresh parsley

¼ cup finely chopped
fresh basil

2 cloves garlic, minced

2 teaspoons salt

¼ teaspoon black pepper

1 pound ground beef

1 pound ground pork

SAUCE

2 tablespoons olive oil

2 tablespoons butter

1 cup finely chopped
yellow onion

1 clove garlic, minced

1 can (28 ounces) whole
Italian plum tomatoes,
coarsely chopped,
juice reserved

1 can (28 ounces)
crushed tomatoes

1 teaspoon salt

¼ teaspoon black pepper

¼ cup finely chopped
fresh basil

1 to 1½ cups ricotta cheese

1 Preheat oven to 375°F. Brush 2 tablespoons oil over large rimmed baking sheet.

2 Combine bread crumbs and milk in large bowl; mix well. Add 1 cup yellow onion, green onions, ½ cup Romano, eggs, parsley, ¼ cup basil, 2 cloves garlic, 2 teaspoons salt and ¼ teaspoon black pepper; mix well. Add beef and pork; mix gently but thoroughly until blended. Shape mixture by ¼ cupfuls into balls. Place meatballs on prepared baking sheet; turn to coat with oil.

3 Bake about 20 minutes or until meatballs are cooked through (160°F). Meanwhile, prepare sauce.

4 Heat 2 tablespoons oil and butter in large saucepan over medium heat until butter is melted. Add 1 cup yellow onion; cook 8 minutes or until tender and lightly browned, stirring frequently. Add 1 clove garlic; cook and stir 1 minute or until fragrant. Add plum tomatoes with juice, crushed tomatoes, 1 teaspoon salt and ¼ teaspoon black pepper; bring to a simmer. Reduce heat to medium-low; cook 20 minutes, stirring occasionally.

5 Stir ¼ cup basil into sauce. Add meatballs; cook 10 minutes, stirring occasionally. Transfer meatballs and sauce to serving dish; dollop tablespoonfuls of ricotta between meatballs. Garnish with additional Romano.

RENEGADE STEAK
MAKES 2 SERVINGS

1½ teaspoons coarse salt

½ teaspoon paprika

½ teaspoon black pepper

¼ teaspoon onion powder

¼ teaspoon garlic powder

⅛ teaspoon ground
   turmeric

⅛ teaspoon ground
   red pepper

⅛ teaspoon ground
   coriander

2 center-cut sirloin,
   strip or tri-tip steaks
   (about 8 ounces each)

2 tablespoons vegetable
   oil

1 tablespoon butter

1 Combine salt, paprika, black pepper, onion powder, garlic powder, turmeric, red pepper and coriander in small bowl; mix well.

2 Season both sides of steaks with spice mixture (you will not need all of it); let steaks stand at room temperature 45 minutes before cooking.

3 Heat large cast iron skillet over high heat. Add oil; heat until oil shimmers and just begins to smoke. Add steaks to skillet; cook 30 seconds, then turn steaks. Cook 30 seconds, then turn again. Continue cooking and turning every 30 seconds for 4 minutes or until golden brown crust begins to form.

4 Add butter to skillet; continue cooking and turning steaks every 30 seconds for 1 minute or until 130° to 135°F for medium rare* or to desired doneness. Remove to plate; let steaks rest 5 minutes before serving.

*Timing given is approximate for 1½-inch steaks; thinner steaks will take less time to cook.

MEATLOAF
MAKES 6 TO 8 SERVINGS

1 tablespoon vegetable oil

2 green onions, minced

¼ cup minced green bell pepper

¼ cup grated carrot

3 cloves garlic, minced

¾ cup milk

2 eggs, beaten

1 pound ground beef

1 pound ground pork

1 cup plain dry bread crumbs

2 teaspoons salt

½ teaspoon onion powder

½ teaspoon black pepper

½ cup ketchup, divided

1 Preheat oven to 350°F.

2 Heat oil in large skillet over medium-high heat. Add green onions, bell pepper, carrot and garlic; cook and stir 5 minutes or until vegetables are softened. Remove from heat.

3 Beat milk and eggs in medium bowl until well blended. Gently mix beef, pork, bread crumbs, salt, onion powder and black pepper in large bowl with hands. Add milk mixture, sautéed vegetables and ¼ cup ketchup; mix gently.

4 Press mixture into 9×5-inch loaf pan; place pan on rimmed baking sheet.

5 Bake 30 minutes. Spread remaining ¼ cup ketchup over meatloaf; bake 1 hour or until cooked through (160°F). Cool in pan 10 minutes before slicing.

HEARTY POTATO AND SAUSAGE BAKE
MAKES 4 TO 6 SERVINGS

1 pound new red potatoes, cut into halves or quarters

1 onion, sliced

8 ounces carrots, cut into 3-inch sticks, *or* baby carrots

2 tablespoons butter, melted

1 teaspoon salt

1 teaspoon garlic powder

½ teaspoon dried thyme

½ teaspoon black pepper

1 pound cooked sausage, cut into ¼-inch slices

1 Preheat oven to 400°F. Spray 13×9-inch baking dish with nonstick cooking spray.

2 Combine potatoes, onion, carrots, butter, salt, garlic powder, thyme and pepper in large bowl; toss to coat. Transfer to prepared baking dish.

3 Bake 30 minutes. Add sausage; mix well. Bake 15 to 20 minutes or until potatoes are tender and golden brown.

HERBED PORK WITH POTATOES AND GREEN BEANS
MAKES 4 SERVINGS

2 tablespoons chopped
   fresh thyme

2 tablespoons chopped
   fresh rosemary

2 cloves garlic, minced

2 teaspoons salt

¾ teaspoon black pepper

¼ cup olive oil

1½ pounds fingerling
   potatoes (about
   18 potatoes), cut
   in half lengthwise

1 pound green beans

2 pork tenderloins (about
   12 ounces each)

1 Preheat oven to 450°F. Combine thyme, rosemary, garlic, salt and pepper in small bowl. Stir in oil until well blended.

2 Place potatoes in medium bowl. Drizzle with one third of oil mixture, toss to coat. Arrange potatoes, cut sides down, in rows covering two thirds of large baking sheet. (Potatoes should be in single layer; do not overlap.) Leave remaining one third of baking sheet empty.

3 Roast potatoes 10 minutes while preparing beans and pork. Trim green beans; place in same bowl used for potatoes. Drizzle with one third of oil mixture; toss to coat.

4 When potatoes have roasted 10 minutes, remove baking sheet from oven. Arrange green beans on empty one third of baking sheet. Brush all sides of pork with remaining oil mixture; place on top of green beans.

5 Roast 20 to 25 minutes or until pork is 145°F. Remove pork to cutting board; tent with foil and let stand 10 minutes. Stir vegetables; return to oven. Roast 10 minutes or until potatoes are dark golden brown and beans are charred in spots. Slice pork; serve with vegetables.

MONGOLIAN BEEF
MAKES 4 SERVINGS

1¼ pounds beef flank steak

¼ cup cornstarch

3 tablespoons vegetable
oil, divided

3 cloves garlic, minced

2 teaspoons grated
fresh ginger

½ cup water

½ cup soy sauce

⅓ cup packed dark
brown sugar

Pinch red pepper flakes

2 green onions, cut
diagonally into
1-inch slices

Hot cooked rice
(optional)

1 Cut flank steak in half lengthwise, then cut
crosswise (against the grain) into ¼-inch slices.

2 Combine beef and cornstarch in medium bowl;
toss to coat.

3 Heat 1 tablespoon oil in large skillet or wok
over high heat. Add half of beef in single layer
(do not crowd); cook 1 to 2 minutes per side or
until browned. Remove to clean bowl. Repeat
with remaining beef and 1 tablespoon oil.

4 Heat remaining 1 tablespoon oil in same
skillet over medium heat. Add garlic and
ginger; cook and stir 30 seconds. Add water,
soy sauce, brown sugar and red pepper flakes;
bring to a boil, stirring until well blended. Cook
8 minutes or until sauce is slightly thickened,
stirring occasionally.

5 Return beef to skillet; cook 2 to 3 minutes
or until sauce thickens and beef is heated
through. Stir in green onions. Serve with
rice, if desired.

DEEP DISH SAUSAGE AND SPINACH PIZZA
MAKES 4 TO 6 SERVINGS

1 loaf (16 ounces) frozen bread dough, thawed according to package directions

8 ounces bulk Italian sausage

⅔ cup pizza sauce

1½ cups (6 ounces) shredded mozzarella cheese

1 package (10 ounces) frozen chopped spinach, thawed and squeezed dry

½ cup grated Parmesan cheese

1 Spray clean work surface with nonstick cooking spray; roll out dough into 12-inch circle. Cover with plastic wrap; let rest 30 minutes.

2 Meanwhile, cook sausage in medium skillet over medium-high heat 8 minutes or until browned, stirring to break up meat. Drain fat. Stir in pizza sauce.

3 Preheat oven to 450°F. Position oven rack near bottom of oven. Spray 9-inch cake pan with cooking spray.

4 Place dough in prepared pan, pressing into bottom and 1 to 1½ inches up side of pan. Sprinkle half of mozzarella over dough; layer with half of sausage mixture, half of spinach, half of Parmesan, remaining half of sausage mixture and spinach. Top with remaining mozzarella and Parmesan.

5 Bake 15 to 18 minutes or until crust is golden brown and cheese is melted and beginning to brown in spots. Cool in pan on wire rack 5 minutes before cutting into wedges.

KALUA PIG
MAKES 6 TO 8 SERVINGS

3 slices bacon

1½ tablespoons coarse sea salt

1 boneless pork shoulder roast (5 to 6 pounds)

1 tablespoon liquid smoke

Hot cooked rice (optional)

Optional toppings: shredded cabbage, sliced green onion, chopped fresh cilantro and fresh pineapple wedges

SLOW COOKER DIRECTIONS

1 Line slow cooker with bacon. Rub salt generously over pork; place on top of bacon. Drizzle liquid smoke over pork.

2 Cover; cook on LOW 16 to 18 hours. Remove pork to large cutting board; shred with two forks. (Do not shred pork in cooking liquid.)

3 Serve pork with rice and desired toppings.

TACO SALAD SUPREME
MAKES 4 SERVINGS

CHILI

1 pound ground beef

1 medium onion, chopped

1 stalk celery, chopped

2 medium fresh tomatoes, chopped

1 jalapeño pepper, finely chopped

1½ teaspoons chili powder

1 teaspoon salt

1 teaspoon ground cumin

½ teaspoon black pepper

1 can (15 ounces) tomato sauce

1 can (about 15 ounces) kidney beans, rinsed and drained

1 can (about 15 ounces) pinto beans, rinsed and drained

1 cup water

SALAD

8 cups chopped romaine lettuce (large pieces)

2 cups diced fresh tomatoes

48 small round tortilla chips

1 cup salsa

½ cup sour cream

½ cup (2 ounces) shredded Cheddar cheese

1 For chili, combine beef, onion and celery in large saucepan; cook over medium-high heat 6 to 8 minutes or until beef is no longer pink, stirring to break up meat. Drain fat.

2 Add chopped tomatoes, jalapeño, chili powder, salt, cumin and black pepper; cook and stir 1 minute. Stir in tomato sauce, beans and water; bring to a boil. Reduce heat to medium-low; cook 1 hour or until most of liquid is absorbed, stirring occasionally.

3 For each salad, combine 2 cups lettuce and ½ cup diced tomatoes in individual bowl. Top with 12 tortilla chips, 1 cup chili, ¼ cup salsa and 2 tablespoons sour cream. Sprinkle with 2 tablespoons cheese. (Reserve remaining chili for another use.)

EASY WEEKEND POT ROAST
MAKES 6 TO 8 SERVINGS

1 boneless beef chuck
  pot roast (about
  3 pounds)

1 teaspoon black pepper

½ teaspoon salt

4 slices bacon, chopped

1 tablespoon olive oil

1 medium onion, sliced

8 ounces sliced
  mushrooms

1 medium green bell
  pepper, coarsely
  chopped

1½ cups pasta sauce

½ cup dry red wine

1½ tablespoons
   balsamic vinegar

1 tablespoon
  Worcestershire
  sauce

1 Preheat oven to 350°F. Sprinkle both sides
  of beef with black pepper and salt.

2 Cook bacon in Dutch oven over medium-high
  heat until until crisp. Drain on paper towel-
  lined plate. Add beef to Dutch oven; cook
  3 to 4 minutes per side or until well browned.
  Remove to plate with bacon. Drain fat.

3 Add oil and onion to Dutch oven; cook and
  stir 4 minutes or until onion is translucent,
  scraping up browned bits from bottom
  of pan. Add mushrooms and bell pepper;
  cook and stir 2 minutes. Remove from heat;
  place beef and bacon on top of vegetables.

4 Combine pasta sauce, wine, vinegar and
  Worcestershire sauce in medium bowl;
  mix well. Pour over beef in Dutch oven.

5 Cover and bake 2½ hours or until beef is
  very tender.

CIDER PORK AND ONIONS
MAKES 8 SERVINGS

2 to 3 tablespoons vegetable oil

4 to 4½ pounds bone-in pork shoulder roast

4 to 5 medium onions, sliced (about 4 cups)

1 teaspoon salt, divided

4 cloves garlic, minced

3 sprigs fresh rosemary

½ teaspoon black pepper

2 to 3 cups apple cider

1 Preheat oven to 325°F. Heat 2 tablespoons oil in Dutch oven over medium-high heat. Add pork; cook until browned on all sides. Remove to plate.

2 Add onions and ½ teaspoon salt to Dutch oven; cook 10 minutes or until translucent, stirring occasionally and adding additional oil as needed to prevent scorching. Add garlic; cook and stir 1 minute.

3 Return pork to Dutch oven with rosemary; sprinkle with remaining ½ teaspoon salt and pepper. Add cider to come about halfway up sides of pork.

4 Cover and bake 2 to 2½ hours or until pork is very tender. (Meat should be almost falling off bones.) Remove to platter; tent with foil to keep warm.

5 Remove and discard rosemary sprigs. Boil liquid in Dutch oven over medium-high heat about 20 minutes or until reduced by half; skim off fat. Season with additional salt and pepper, if desired. Cut pork; serve with sauce.

STEAK FAJITAS
MAKES 2 SERVINGS

¼ cup lime juice

¼ cup soy sauce

4 tablespoons vegetable oil, divided

2 tablespoons honey

2 tablespoons Worcestershire sauce

2 cloves garlic, minced

½ teaspoon ground red pepper

1 pound flank steak, skirt steak or top sirloin

1 medium yellow onion, halved and cut into ¼-inch slices

1 green bell pepper, cut into ¼-inch strips

1 red bell pepper, cut into ¼-inch strips

Flour tortillas, warmed

Lime wedges (optional)

Optional toppings: pico de gallo, guacamole, sour cream, shredded lettuce and shredded Cheddar-Jack cheese

1 Whisk lime juice, soy sauce, 2 tablespoons oil, honey, Worcestershire sauce, garlic and ground red pepper in medium bowl until well blended. Pour ¼ cup marinade into large bowl.

2 Place steak in large resealable food storage bag. Pour remaining marinade over steak; seal bag and turn to coat. Marinate in refrigerator at least 2 hours or overnight. Add onion and bell peppers to bowl with ¼ cup marinade; toss to coat. Cover and refrigerate until ready to use.

3 Remove steak from marinade; discard marinade. Pat steak dry with paper towels. Heat 1 tablespoon oil in large skillet (preferably cast iron) over medium-high heat. Cook steak 4 minutes per side for medium rare or to desired doneness. Remove to cutting board; tent with foil and let stand 10 minutes.

4 Meanwhile, heat remaining 1 tablespoon oil in same skillet over medium-high heat. Add vegetable mixture; cook 8 minutes or until vegetables are crisp-tender and beginning to brown in spots, stirring occasionally. (Cook in two batches if necessary; do not crowd vegetables in skillet.)

5 Cut steak into thin slices across the grain. Serve with vegetables, tortillas, lime wedges and desired toppings.

JAMAICAN JERK PORK CHOPS
MAKES 4 SERVINGS

2 green onions, minced

Juice and peel from 2 medium limes

2 to 3 tablespoons jerk seasoning

2 tablespoons olive oil

1½ tablespoons soy sauce

2 cloves garlic, minced

1½ teaspoons sugar

¼ teaspoon salt

4 thick-cut bone-in pork chops (about 8 ounces each)

1 Combine green onions, lime juice, lime peel, jerk seasoning, oil, soy sauce, garlic, sugar and salt in medium bowl; mix well. Place pork chops in large resealable food storage bag. Add green onion mixture; seal bag and turn to coat. Refrigerate overnight, turning occasionally.

2 Preheat broiler and broiler pan. Spray broiler pan with nonstick cooking spray (away from heat source). Remove pork chops from marinade; discard marinade.

3 Broil pork chops 4 inches from heat source 4 to 6 minutes per side or until pork is barely pink in center.

SMOKED SAUSAGE WITH SAUERKRAUT AND APPLES
MAKES 4 TO 6 SERVINGS

2 pounds refrigerated sauerkraut

1 tablespoon vegetable oil

2 Granny Smith apples, peeled and cut into ½-inch wedges

1 medium onion, chopped

1 cup lager

1 tablespoon packed brown sugar

1½ teaspoons caraway seeds (optional)

1½ pounds smoked sausages, such as kielbasa

Black pepper

1 Preheat oven to 325°F.

2 Drain sauerkraut; rinse under cold water and drain again. Squeeze out excess liquid.

3 Heat oil in large ovenproof skillet over medium heat. Add apples; cook and stir 2 minutes or until lightly browned. Add onion; cook and stir 6 minutes or until golden brown. Stir in sauerkraut, lager, brown sugar and caraway seeds, if desired; bring to a boil.

4 Pierce sausages with fork; add to skillet and cover with sauerkraut mixture. Cover skillet, leaving lid slightly ajar.

5 Bake 30 minutes or until sausages are heated through and most liquid has evaporated. Season sauerkraut with pepper. Serve immediately.

BEEF POT PIE
MAKES 4 TO 6 SERVINGS

½ cup all-purpose flour

1 teaspoon salt, divided

½ teaspoon black pepper, divided

1½ pounds lean beef stew meat (1-inch pieces)

2 tablespoons olive oil

1 pound unpeeled new red potatoes, cubed

2 cups baby carrots

1 cup frozen pearl onions, thawed

1 parsnip, peeled and cut into 1-inch pieces

1 cup stout

¾ cup beef broth

1 teaspoon chopped fresh thyme *or* ½ teaspoon dried thyme

1 refrigerated pie crust (half of 14-ounce package)

1 Preheat oven to 350°F. Combine flour, ½ teaspoon salt and ¼ teaspoon pepper in large resealable food storage bag. Add beef; shake to coat.

2 Heat oil in large skillet over medium-high heat. Add beef; cook until browned on all sides. (Do not crowd beef; cook in batches if necessary.) Transfer to 2½- to 3-quart casserole. Stir in potatoes, carrots, onions and parsnip.

3 Add stout, broth, thyme, remaining ½ teaspoon salt and ¼ teaspoon pepper to skillet; bring to a boil, scraping up browned bits from bottom of skillet. Pour over beef and vegetables in casserole; mix well.

4 Cover and bake 2½ to 3 hours or until beef is fork-tender, stirring once. Uncover; let stand at room temperature 15 minutes. *Increase oven temperature to 425°F.*

5 Place pie crust over casserole and press edges to seal. Cut slits in crust to vent.

6 Bake 15 to 20 minutes or until crust is golden brown. Cool slightly before serving.

SPICY PORK STIR-FRY
MAKES 4 SERVINGS

¼ cup water

2 teaspoons cornstarch

4 tablespoons peanut oil, divided

6 whole dried hot red chile peppers

4 cloves garlic, sliced

1 pork tenderloin (about 12 ounces), thinly sliced

1 large carrot, cut into ¼-inch-thick slices

2 ounces fresh oyster, shiitake or button mushrooms,* cut into halves

1 baby eggplant, thinly sliced

5 ounces fresh snow peas, ends trimmed

3 tablespoons packed brown sugar

2 tablespoons fish sauce

1 tablespoon dark sesame oil

Hot cooked rice (optional)

*Or substitute ½ ounce dried shiitake mushrooms, soaked according to package directions.

1 Stir water into cornstarch in small bowl until well blended; set aside.

2 Heat wok or large skillet over high heat 1 minute. Drizzle 2 tablespoons peanut oil into wok; heat 30 seconds. Add chile peppers and garlic; stir-fry 30 seconds. Add pork; stir-fry 3 to 4 minutes or until barely pink in center. Remove pork mixture to medium bowl.

3 Add remaining 2 tablespoons peanut oil to wok. Add carrot, mushrooms and eggplant; stir-fry 2 minutes. Add snow peas and pork mixture; stir-fry 1 minute.

4 Stir cornstarch mixture; add to wok. Cook 1 minute or until sauce thickens. Stir in brown sugar, fish sauce and sesame oil; cook and stir until heated through. Serve with rice, if desired.

MUSTARD–CRUSTED RIB ROAST
MAKES 6 TO 8 SERVINGS

1 (3-rib) beef rib roast, trimmed* (6 to 7 pounds)

3 tablespoons Dijon mustard

1½ tablespoons chopped fresh tarragon *or* 1½ teaspoons dried tarragon

3 cloves garlic, minced

¼ cup dry red wine

⅓ cup finely chopped shallots

1 tablespoon all-purpose flour

1 cup beef broth

*Ask butcher to remove chine bone for easier carving. Trim fat to ¼-inch thickness.

1 Preheat oven to 450°F. Place roast, bone side down, in shallow roasting pan. Combine mustard, tarragon and garlic in small bowl; mix well. Spread over all sides of roast except bottom.

2 Roast 10 minutes. *Reduce oven temperature to 350°F.* Roast 1½ to 2 hours for medium rare (125° to 130°F) or to desired doneness. (Internal temperature of roast will continue to rise 5° to 10°F as it rests.)

3 Remove roast to cutting board; tent with foil and let stand 20 minutes before carving.

4 Reserve 1 tablespoon drippings in medium saucepan; drain off and discard remaining drippings. Add wine to roasting pan; place over two burners on stovetop. Cook over medium heat 2 minutes or until reduced and slightly thickened, scraping up browned bits from bottom of pan.

5 Add shallots to reserved drippings in saucepan; cook and stir over medium heat 4 minutes or until softened. Add flour; cook and stir 1 minute. Add broth and wine mixture from roasting pan; cook 5 minutes or until sauce thickens, stirring occasionally. Strain into serving dish, pressing on shallots with back of spoon.

6 Cut roast into ½-inch-thick slices. Serve with gravy.

SIMPLE SALSA STEAK
MAKES 4 SERVINGS

1½ cups medium salsa

3 tablespoons lime juice

1½ tablespoons olive oil

¾ teaspoon chipotle
   chili powder

¾ teaspoon ground cumin

1½ pounds flank steak

1 green onion, finely
  chopped

1 Combine salsa, lime juice, oil, chili powder and cumin in large resealable food storage bag; mix well. Reserve half of mixture for serving; set aside. Add steak to bag; seal bag to coat and massage marinade into steak. Marinate in refrigerator at least 2 hours or overnight.

2 Preheat broiler. Line baking sheet or broiler pan with foil. Remove steak from marinade; discard marinade. Brush off any large pieces of marinade from steak; place on prepared baking sheet.

3 Broil steak about 5 minutes per side or until desired doneness (130° to 135°F for medium rare). Let stand 5 minutes before slicing against the grain.

4 Stir green onion into reserved salsa mixture; serve with steak.

SPANISH PAELLA WITH CHICKEN AND SAUSAGE
MAKES 4 SERVINGS

1 tablespoon olive oil

4 chicken thighs
(about 2 pounds)

1 onion, chopped

1 clove garlic, minced

4 cups chicken broth

1 pound hot smoked
sausage, cut into
½-inch slices

1 can (about 14 ounces)
stewed tomatoes,
undrained

1 cup uncooked
arborio rice

1 pinch saffron threads
(optional)

½ cup frozen peas, thawed

SLOW COOKER DIRECTIONS

1 Heat oil in large skillet over medium-high heat.
Add chicken; cook 4 to 5 minutes per side or
until browned. Remove to slow cooker.

2 Add onion to skillet; cook and stir 4 minutes
or until translucent, scraping up browned
bits from bottom of skillet. Add garlic; cook
and stir 30 seconds. Stir in broth, sausage,
tomatoes, rice and saffron, if desired; mix
well. Pour over chicken.

3 Cover; cook on LOW 6 to 8 hours or on HIGH
3 to 4 hours or until chicken is cooked through
and rice is tender.

4 Transfer chicken to plate. Stir peas into rice
mixture in slow cooker; cover and let stand
2 minutes or until heated through. Spoon
rice into serving bowls; top with chicken.

TRI-TIP ROAST WITH SPICY POTATOES
MAKES 4 TO 6 SERVINGS

4 teaspoons chili powder

2 teaspoons dried oregano

1 teaspoon salt

3 pounds unpeeled
round red potatoes
(about 9 medium)

3 tablespoons lime juice,
divided

1 tablespoon olive oil

1 boneless beef loin tri-tip
roast (about 2 pounds)

1 Preheat oven to 450°F. Spray 13×9-inch baking dish with nonstick cooking spray. Combine chili powder, oregano and salt in small bowl; mix well.

2 Cut potatoes into wedges; place in large bowl. Add 2 tablespoons lime juice, oil and 1 tablespoon spice mixture; toss to coat. Spread potatoes in single layer in prepared baking dish.

3 Brush roast with remaining 1 tablespoon lime juice; rub with remaining spice mixture. Place roast on rack in roasting pan.

4 Roast 10 minutes. Place potatoes beside or below roast in oven; roast 30 to 40 minutes or until potatoes are tender and browned and beef is 125° to 130°F for medium rare. Tent beef and potatoes with foil; let roast stand 10 minutes before carving.

5 Cut roast into thin slices against the grain; serve with potatoes.

SWEET AND SAVORY BEEF BRISKET
MAKES 6 SERVINGS

1 large onion, thinly sliced

1 small (2 to 2½ pounds) beef brisket

1 teaspoon salt

½ teaspoon black pepper

⅔ cup chili sauce, divided

1½ tablespoons packed brown sugar

¼ teaspoon ground cinnamon

2 large sweet potatoes, peeled and cut into 1-inch pieces

1 cup (5 ounces) pitted prunes

2 tablespoons cornstarch

2 tablespoons cold water

SLOW COOKER DIRECTIONS

1 Place onion in slow cooker. Arrange brisket over onion (tucking edges under to fit, if necessary). Sprinkle with salt and pepper; top with ⅓ cup chili sauce.

2 Cover; cook on HIGH 3½ hours. Meanwhile, combine remaining ⅓ cup chili sauce, brown sugar and cinnamon in large bowl. Add sweet potatoes and prunes; toss to coat.

3 Spoon chili sauce mixture over brisket. Cover; cook on HIGH 1¼ to 1½ hours or until brisket and sweet potatoes are tender. Remove brisket to cutting board; tent with foil. Transfer sweet potato mixture to serving platter with slotted spoon, leaving juices in slow cooker. Cover to keep warm.

4 Stir cornstarch into water in small bowl until smooth. Stir into liquid in slow cooker; mix well. Cover; cook on HIGH 10 minutes or until sauce thickens.

5 Cut brisket into thin slices against the grain; serve with sweet potato mixture and sauce.

ROASTED SAUSAGE WITH WHITE BEANS
MAKES 4 SERVINGS

1 pound mild or hot
   Italian sausage

2 tablespoons extra virgin
   olive oil

10 fresh sage leaves
   (about 1 sprig)

2 cloves garlic, minced

1 can (about 14 ounces)
   diced tomatoes

2 cans (about 15 ounces
   each) cannellini beans,
   rinsed and drained

¼ teaspoon salt

⅛ teaspoon black pepper

1 Preheat oven to 400°F. Line rimmed baking sheet with foil. Arrange sausages on prepared baking sheet; roast about 18 minutes or until sausages are cooked through.

2 Meanwhile, heat oil in large skillet over medium-low heat. Add sage and garlic; cook 2 to 3 minutes or just until garlic begins to turn golden. Add tomatoes; bring to a simmer.

3 Stir in beans, salt and pepper; cook 15 minutes, stirring occasionally. Serve sausages over beans.

NOTE

Sausages can be grilled instead of roasted.

PORK CHOPS WITH VINEGAR PEPPERS
MAKES 4 SERVINGS

4 pork rib chops
  (about 1 inch thick)

½ teaspoon salt

¼ teaspoon black pepper

2 tablespoons olive oil

1½ cups seeded hot cherry
  peppers, cut into
  ½-inch slices*

2 cloves garlic, minced

¼ cup liquid from
  cherry pepper jar

¼ cup water

1 sprig fresh rosemary

  Chopped fresh Italian
  parsley (optional)

*Hot cherry peppers are also
available presliced in rings.

1 Pat pork chops dry with paper towels. Season both sides with salt and black pepper.

2 Heat oil in large skillet over medium-high heat. Add pork chops; cook about 5 minutes per side or until browned. Remove to plate; keep warm.

3 Add cherry peppers and garlic to skillet; cook and stir 2 minutes over medium heat, scraping up browned bits from bottom of skillet. Stir in cherry pepper liquid, water and rosemary.

4 Return pork chops to skillet; cover and cook about 6 minutes or until pork is barely pink in center. Sprinkle with parsley, if desired.

THAI STEAK AND HERB SALAD WITH MIXED GRAINS
MAKES 4 SERVINGS

½ cup *each* millet and quinoa, rinsed well in sieve

2 cups water

¼ cup plus 1 tablespoon vegetable oil, divided

1 pound flank steak

Kosher salt and freshly ground black pepper

¼ cup minced shallots

2 tablespoons fish sauce

2 tablespoons lime juice

2 teaspoons packed brown sugar

1 head romaine lettuce, chopped

1 cup loosely packed fresh cilantro leaves

1 cup cherry tomatoes, halved

½ cup *each* julienned fresh mint and basil leaves

4 radishes, thinly sliced

½ cup roasted salted peanuts

1 Combine millet, quinoa and water in small saucepan over high heat; bring to a boil over high heat. Reduce heat to low; cover and cook about 20 minutes or until grains are tender.

2 Meanwhile, heat 1 tablespoon oil in large skillet over medium-high heat. Season steak generously with salt and pepper on both sides.

3 Cook steak 3 to 4 minutes per side for medium rare or to desired doneness. Remove steak to cutting board; let stand 10 minutes before cutting into thin slices against the grain.

4 Whisk shallots, fish sauce, lime juice, brown sugar and remaining ¼ cup oil in small bowl until well blended.

5 Combine cooked grains, lettuce, cilantro, tomatoes, mint, basil and radishes in large bowl. Top with steak and peanuts; serve with dressing.

INDEX

INDEX

METRIC CONVERSION CHART

VOLUME MEASUREMENTS (dry)

1/8 teaspoon = 0.5 mL
1/4 teaspoon = 1 mL
1/2 teaspoon = 2 mL
3/4 teaspoon = 4 mL
1 teaspoon = 5 mL
1 tablespoon = 15 mL
2 tablespoons = 30 mL
1/4 cup = 60 mL
1/3 cup = 75 mL
1/2 cup = 125 mL
2/3 cup = 150 mL
3/4 cup = 175 mL
1 cup = 250 mL
2 cups = 1 pint = 500 mL
3 cups = 750 mL
4 cups = 1 quart = 1 L

VOLUME MEASUREMENTS (fluid)

1 fluid ounce (2 tablespoons) = 30 mL
4 fluid ounces (1/2 cup) = 125 mL
8 fluid ounces (1 cup) = 250 mL
12 fluid ounces (1 1/2 cups) = 375 mL
16 fluid ounces (2 cups) = 500 mL

WEIGHTS (mass)

1/2 ounce = 15 g
1 ounce = 30 g
3 ounces = 90 g
4 ounces = 120 g
8 ounces = 225 g
10 ounces = 285 g
12 ounces = 360 g
16 ounces = 1 pound = 450 g

DIMENSIONS

1/16 inch = 2 mm
1/8 inch = 3 mm
1/4 inch = 6 mm
1/2 inch = 1.5 cm
3/4 inch = 2 cm
1 inch = 2.5 cm

OVEN TEMPERATURES

250°F = 120°C
275°F = 140°C
300°F = 150°C
325°F = 160°C
350°F = 180°C
375°F = 190°C
400°F = 200°C
425°F = 220°C
450°F = 230°C

BAKING PAN SIZES

Utensil	Size in Inches/Quarts	Metric Volume	Size in Centimeters
Baking or Cake Pan (square or rectangular)	8×8×2	2 L	20×20×5
	9×9×2	2.5 L	23×23×5
	12×8×2	3 L	30×20×5
	13×9×2	3.5 L	33×23×5
Loaf Pan	8×4×3	1.5 L	20×10×7
	9×5×3	2 L	23×13×7
Round Layer Cake Pan	8×1½	1.2 L	20×4
	9×1½	1.5 L	23×4
Pie Plate	8×1¼	750 mL	20×3
	9×1¼	1 L	23×3
Baking Dish or Casserole	1 quart	1 L	—
	1½ quart	1.5 L	—
	2 quart	2 L	—